CONNECTICUT
TRIVIA

CONNECTICUT TRIVIA

Compiled by Frank Abate

Rutledge Hill Press®

Nashville, Tennessee

A Thomas Nelson Company

Published by Rutledge Hill Press, a Division of Thomas Nelson, Inc., P.O. Box 141000, Nashville, Tennessee 37214.

Library of Congress Cataloging-in-Publication Data Available

Abate, Frank R.
  Connecticut trivia / compiled by Frank Abate.
      p. cm.
  ISBN 1-55853-925-5
 1. Connecticut—Miscellanea. 2. Questions and answers. I. Title.
  F94.6 .A33 2001
  974.6'0076—dc21

2001002904

Printed in the United States of America

1 2 3 4 5 6 7—05 04 03 02 01

PREFACE

We are very pleased to offer you *Connecticut Trivia* with more than 1,200 facts and features of Connecticut. Connecticut, known as The Nutmeg State for its unscrupulous vendors of wooden nutmegs, The Constitution State for the first written constitution: Hartford's Fundamental Orders of 1639, and The Provision State for the troops supplied during the Revolutionary War, has a long and cherished history. Native Americans lived along Connecticut's shore and rivers 10,000 years ago. The first Europeans arrived in 1614, as Dutch explorer Adriaen Block sailed along the coast and up the Connecticut River, which he called the *Versche* ("Fresh") for its cold, clean water. English colonists arrived in the early 1630s, settling in present-day Hartford, Windsor, Wethersfield, and Old Saybrook. Reflections of colonial days still abound in Connecticut, with its many Congregational churches, its historic homes and museums, its strong ties to the sea, and the independent character of Connecticut's 169 towns and cities.

Connecticut Trivia presents "the best and the brightest" from all around the state. I take full responsibility for any errors or oversights, and welcome corrections and suggestions. Please feel free to write to me care of Rutledge Hill Press.

Rutledge Hill Press
P.O. Box 141000
Nashville, TN 37214

To Ali, Greg, and Philip:

Carissimi, hoc libellum ad vos mitto.

TABLE OF CONTENTS

GEOGRAPHY

C H A P T E R O N E

Q. In what year did explorer Adriaen Block first explore the Connecticut coast?

A. 1614.

Q. How many commercial vineyards are located within the state of Connecticut?

A. Nine.

Q. At what Connecticut school was famed financier J. Pierpont Morgan once a student?

A. Cheshire Academy.

Q. How many times would a state the size of Connecticut fit into the land area of Alaska?

A. 116.

Q. In what Connecticut town are all Mounds and Almond Joy candy bars made?

A. Naugatuck.

Q. What was the Native American name for the area now called East Hartford?

A. Podunk.

Q. What Connecticut town supplied much of the brownstone for New York City apartment buildings?

A. Portland.

Q. How many dogwood trees are estimated to be growing in the town of Fairfield?

A. Thirty thousand.

Q. How much water can be provided by the West Hartford Reservoir on a daily basis?

A. Fifty million gallons.

Q. By what other descriptive name is the panhandle of Connecticut known?

A. The handle of the cleaver.

Q. What borough is Connecticut's smallest municipality, with a total population of fifty-two in 2000?

A. Fenwick (part of Old Saybrook).

Q. What Hartford park boasts the first municipal rose garden in the United States?

A. Elizabeth Park.

Q. What city was co-capital of Connecticut along with Hartford from 1701 to 1875?

A. New Haven.

Q. What Connecticut town seceded from the Massachusetts Bay Colony in 1749?

A. Enfield.

Q. Carbon-dated archeological evidence suggests that Native Americans occupied Connecticut at least how many years ago?

A. Ten thousand.

Q. Under the Connecticut Charter (1662) what was Connecticut's western boundary?

A. The Pacific Ocean.

Q. Coginchaug, the Native American name for the area now called Durham, means what?

A. Long Swamp.

Q. What is Connecticut's most valuable single food crop?

A. Mushrooms.

Q. What Connecticut town has a name used by no other municipality in America?

A. Bozrah.

Q. What is designated as Connecticut's state shellfish?

A. The eastern oyster (*Crassostrea virginica*).

Q. Danbury was long the national center for a certain industry, and so was known by what nickname?

A. The Hat City.

Q. In what year was New Haven Green and the surrounding downtown area laid out?

A. 1639.

Q. What is the name of the boat that is used for the Chester-Hadlyme Ferry?

A. Selden III.

Q. What artificial lake is the largest freshwater body in Connecticut?

A. Candlewood Lake.

Q. What crop is grown in north central Connecticut under gauze netting?

A. Shade tobacco (used for cigar wrappers).

Q. What infamous pirate is said to have hidden treasure on Connecticut's Thimble Islands?

A. Captain Kidd.

Q. Gillette Castle is built mainly out of what local material?

A. Fieldstone.

Q. How far upriver do tides occur in the Connecticut River estuary?

A. Sixty miles.

Q. How many cities and towns are there in Connecticut?

A. 169.

Q. How many Connecticut cities have a population of greater than 100,000, according to the 2000 Census?

A. Five (Bridgeport, Hartford, New Haven, Stamford, and Waterbury).

Q. How many covered bridges still remain in the state of Connecticut?

A. Five.

Q. How many different species of birds are said to visit the Audubon Center in Greenwich?

A. 160.

Q. How many justices serve on Connecticut's Supreme Court?

A. Seven.

Q. Besides Connecticut, what other state does not have government at the county level?

A. Rhode Island.

Q. How many lighthouses (operational and historical) are still standing in Connecticut?

A. Eighteen.

Q. What Connecticut town was once known as The Greeting Card Capital of the World?

A. North Branford.

Q. At what city does the Housatonic River empty into Long Island Sound?

A. Bridgeport.

Q. How many Native American Indian reservations are there in Connecticut?

A. Five.

Q. How many present-day towns were once part of the original Saybrook Colony?

A. Seven.

Q. What is the height of Hartford's Civil War memorial, the Soldiers and Sailors Memorial Arch?

A. 116 feet.

Q. What is the state bird of Connecticut?

A. The American robin.

Q. How many state universities are located in Connecticut?

A. Five.

Q. What nickname is sometimes used of the Fairfield County towns that are suburbs of New York City?

A. The Gold Coast.

Q. In prehistoric times, northwestern Connecticut was on the shore of what ocean?

A. Iapetos.

Q. What Connecticut town boasts the largest town green in New England?

A. Guilford.

Q. In what county is the Schaghticoke Indian reservation, the state's smallest?

A. Litchfield County.

Q. What is the Connecticut state motto?

A. Qui transtulit sustinet (Latin: He who transplanted still sustains).

Q. For whom is the town of Clinton, Connecticut, named?

A. New York Gov. Dewitt Clinton, of Erie Canal fame.

Q. In what New England state does the Connecticut River have its source?

A. New Hampshire.

Q. In what year did Connecticut abolish county governments?

A. 1960.

Q. What is the name of the territory, now part of Ohio, that was once part of Connecticut?

A. The Western Reserve.

Q. What is Connecticut's rank among the fifty states in land area?

A. Third smallest.

Q. Bradley International Airport, which serves Hartford, is actually in what town?

A. Windsor Locks.

Q. In what year did floods change the course of the Connecticut River, limiting navigation upstream to Rocky Hill?

A. 1700.

Q. What is the state insect of Connecticut?

A. The praying mantis.

Q. Who is Connecticut's state heroine?

A. Prudence Crandall.

Q. A thirty-two-mile section of what Connecticut state highway was designated a National Scenic Byway in 1996?

A. Route 169 in eastern Connecticut.

Q. Approximately how old do scientists estimate the dinosaur tracks on display at Dinosaur State Park to be?

A. 150 to 200 million years old.

Q. What nickname was long used for East Hampton (known as Chatham before 1915) because of the industry based there?

A. "Bell Town."

Q. What is the height above sea level at Meriden's National Historical Landmark called Castle Craig?

A. 1,002 feet.

Q. In what year was the Saybrook Colony originally settled?

A. 1635.

Q. What Connecticut city is nicknamed the Elm City?

A. New Haven.

Q. Lakes Washining and Washinee in Litchfield County are also known by what name?

A. The Twin Lakes.

Q. What is Connecticut's state fossil?

A. The dinosaur tracks of *Eubrontes giganteus*.

Q. Mansfield is part of what area deeded to the English by Native Americans in 1675?

A. Joshua's Tract.

Q. What is the name of the covered bridge in Kent, one of two in the state still open to vehicles?

A. Bulls Bridge.

Q. Middletown was so named because it was halfway between Saybrook and what other place?

A. Windsor.

Q. New London ferries offer service from New London to what two Long Island destinations?

A. Montauk and Orient Point.

Q. On what date was the Connecticut River designated an American Heritage River?

A. July 30, 1998.

Q. What was the name of the first settlement (1654) in what is now Ansonia?

A. Uptown Derby.

Q. Besides the on-campus Gampel Pavilion, where else do University of Connecticut basketball teams play their home games?

A. Hartford Civic Center.

Q. The *Q* in New Haven's Q Bridge stands for what?

A. Quinnipiac (the river it spans).

Q. The Eastern Wall, the boundary between Connecticut's central valley and eastern uplands, can best be viewed from a lookout tower where?

A. On Soapstone Mountain.

Q. The Farmington Canal (1828–48) ran from Northampton, Massachusetts, and ended where?

A. New Haven.

Q. What Connecticut nickname best reflects its traditional New England character?

A. The Land of Steady Habits.

Q. The first chartered copper mine in the colonies was established in East Granby in what year?

A. 1707.

Q. What is the name of the highway that continues east from the end of the Merritt Parkway?

A. The Wilbur Cross Parkway.

Q. What is the height above sea level of New Haven's West Rock Ridge?

A. 627 feet.

Q. How many major tributaries does the Connecticut River have?

A. Thirty-eight.

Q. What is the length of Connecticut's scenic Merritt Parkway?

A. 37.5 miles.

Q. The first federally operated lighthouse in Connecticut is located in what town?

A. Stonington.

Q. The harbor of Norwalk is a leading East Coast producer of what variety of shellfish?

A. Oyster.

Q. What is the name of the sheer cliffs that jut up from the flat-lands near Meriden?

A. The Hanging Hills.

Q. Named to honor James Madison in 1826, the town of Madison was previously called what?

A. East Guilford.

Q. What river empties into Long Island Sound at New Haven?

A. The Quinnipiac.

Q. The Mashantucket Pequot Reservation, home of Foxwoods Casino, is primarily inside the boundaries of what town?

A. Ledyard.

Q. What was the original name of the town of Farmington?

A. Tunxis.

Q. The village of Mystic actually has portions in what two Connecticut towns?

A. Stonington and Groton.

Q. What is the length of the Metacomet Trail, running from Meriden to the Massachusetts line?

A. Fifty-one miles.

Q. Tobacco cultivation was introduced into Connecticut in 1640 with seed from what other colony?

A. Virginia.

Q. Totoket is the Native American name for the area now called what?

A. North Branford.

Q. What is the height of Heublein Tower atop Talcott Mountain?

A. 165 feet.

Q. East Windsor, Ellington, Enfield, and Somers put on the Four Town Fair, but in which town is the fairgrounds?

A. Somers.

Q. Wangumbaug, the Native American name for the area now known as Coventry, is translated as what?

A. Crooked pond.

Q. What was the original location of New Haven's Yale University, founded in 1701?

A. Saybrook.

Q. Connecticut's municipal governments include cities, towns, and what other entities?

A. Boroughs.

Q. What are the two principal rivers in the northeastern part of Connecticut?

A. The Quinebaug and the Shetucket.

Q. Into what body of water does the Connecticut River empty?

A. Long Island Sound.

Q. In what year was the Thankful Arnold House—now restored and home to the Haddam Historical Society—built?

A. 1794.

Q. By what name was Interstate 95 in Connecticut once commonly known?

A. The Connecticut Turnpike.

Q. What bridge was the longest in New England (3,420 feet) when it opened in 1938?

A. The Arrigoni Bridge (Middletown–Portland).

Q. What town is in Connecticut's northeast corner?

A. Thompson.

Q. What Connecticut city is nicknamed the Hardware City of the World?

A. New Britain (home of the tool company Stanley Works).

Q. What is Connecticut's original telephone area code?

A. 203.

Q. What Connecticut city is the headquarters for the Catholic service organization known as the Knights of Columbus?

A. New Haven.

Q. How many miles of blazed hiking trails are there in Connecticut?

A. Seven hundred.

Q. What Connecticut city was once known as the Silver City of the World as the center of its chief industry?

A. Meriden.

Q. What Connecticut city was the long-time center of America's brass industry?

A. Waterbury.

Q. What is the name of the small beach on Long Island Sound at Stonington Point?

A. Du Bois Beach.

Q. What Connecticut city, home of Yale Lock Co., is nicknamed The Lock City?

A. Stamford.

Q. What is the name of Connecticut's largest airport?

A. Bradley International Airport.

Q. What is the size of Bantam Lake, Connecticut's largest natural lake?

A. 916 acres.

Q. What Connecticut museum was built from local fieldstone, by the Civilian Conservation Corps?

A. The Stone Museum, in Peoples State Forest.

Q. How many miles of stone walls are there said to be throughout Connecticut?

A. Twenty-five thousand.

Q. What bridge connects Hartford and East Hartford via Route 15?

A. The Charter Oak Bridge.

Q. What Connecticut nickname reflects its Puritan heritage?

A. The Blue Law State.

Q. The lighthouse depicted on many Connecticut license plates is located where?

A. Lynde Point, Old Saybrook.

Q. What Connecticut park is the first in the country ever taken by eminent domain for use as a park?

A. Bushnell Park, in Hartford.

Q. What Connecticut town boasts the oldest continuous agricultural fair in the United States, held annually since 1852?

A. Brooklyn.

Q. The Native American tribes of Connecticut are all part of what linguistic group?

A. Algonquian.

Q. What is the state mineral of Connecticut?

A. Garnet.

Q. What was the name of the mining community near West Cornwall, now a ghost town?

A. Dudleytown.

Q. What was the Native American name for the area that is now the site of Hartford?

A. Suckiaug.

Q. How many miles of road were once toll-paying turnpikes in Connecticut?

A. Fourteen hundred.

Q. What is the length of Connecticut's shoreline along Long Island Sound?

A. 253 miles.

Q. What Connecticut town has the highest elevations in the state?

A. Salisbury.

Q. Pioneering U.S. lexicographer Noah Webster was born in what Connecticut town?

A. West Hartford.

Q. What river joins with the Quinebaug near Norwich to form the Thames River?

A. The Yantic.

Q. What is the height of Litchfield County's Mount Tom?

A. 1,291 feet.

Q. What river separates the cities of New London and Groton?

A. The Thames.

Q. What Connecticut town is the largest in land area?

A. Woodstock (60.5 square miles).

Q. What Connecticut town is the smallest in land area?

A. Derby (5 square miles).

Q. In what year was the last stand of virgin forest in Connecticut logged?

A. 1912.

Q. What bridge carries Interstate 95 over the Connecticut River?

A. Raymond E. Baldwin Bridge.

Q. What Connecticut building was the tallest in New England from 1919 until the 1960s?

A. Travelers Tower in Hartford (527 feet).

Q. What Connecticut village is the site of two mineral springs reputed to have curative properties?

A. Stafford Springs.

Q. What county is in Connecticut's northeast corner?

A. Windham.

Q. What is the name of the river that flows into Stamford harbor?

A. The Rippowan.

Q. What crop closely associated with Wethersfield is used as a town symbol?

A. The onion.

Q. What does the name of the river called the Housatonic mean in the Mahican language?

A. Place beyond the mountains.

Q. What body of water lies to Connecticut's south?

A. Long Island Sound.

Q. What early settler from Salem, Massachusetts, named the town of Salem in 1725?

A. Colonel Samuel Browne.

Q. What eastern Connecticut town, home of Pachaug State Forest, is actually over two-thirds state-owned land?

A. Voluntown.

Q. What English captain erected a fort near the mouth of the Connecticut River?

A. Lion Gardiner.

Q. What four towns and cities are in Connecticut's "panhandle" near New York state?

A. Greenwich, Stamford, Darien, and New Canaan.

Q. What is Connecticut's highest-grossing category of agricultural products?

A. Nursery and greenhouse products.

Q. What is Connecticut's largest county in land area?

A. Litchfield (920 square miles).

Q. What is Connecticut's largest county in population?

A. Fairfield (882,567 in the 2000 Census).

Q. What is the name of the twenty-three-mile hiking trail that passes through Sleeping Giant State Park?

A. The Quinnipiac Trail.

Q. What Connecticut town post office is annually a tourist mecca at Christmastime?

A. Bethlehem, Connecticut.

Q. What is Connecticut's rank among the fifty states in density of population?

A. Fourth most densely populated.

Q. What is Connecticut's smallest town in population?

A. Union (693 in the 2000 Census).

Q. What was the Native American name for the area that is now the city of Waterbury?

A. Mattatuck.

Q. What is the total length of the Connecticut River?

A. 410 miles.

Q. What is the name of the large island near the mouth of the Connecticut River?

A. Great Island.

Q. What is Connecticut's state ship?

A. The USS Nautilus.

Q. What is said to be the total number of islands in the Thimble Island group?

A. 365.

Q. What is the exact site of the Connecticut River Museum in Essex?

A. Steamboat Dock.

Q. What Connecticut town, surrounded by apple orchards, has been called "the Little Apple"?

A. Southington.

Q. What is the general direction of Interstate 95 south in Connecticut?

A. West.

Q. What is the height of the granite obelisk at Fort Griswold Battlefield State Park in Groton?

A. 134 feet.

Q. What is the land area (in square miles) of the Connecticut River watershed?

A. Eleven thousand.

Q. What is the length of the beach at Hammonasset State Park in Madison?

A. 2.25 miles.

Q. What is the meaning of Paquiaug, the Native American name for the Danbury area?

A. Cleared land.

Q. What is the most common nickname for Connecticut residents?

A. Nutmeggers.

Q. What is the name for the series of traprock ridges that run down Connecticut's central valley?

A. Metacomet Ridge.

Q. Which state lies immediately to the east of Connecticut?

A. Rhode Island.

Q. What river's mouth is at Connecticut's border with Rhode Island?

A. The Pawcatuck River.

Q. What is the name of Connecticut's only national park, based in Wilton?

A. Weir Farm.

Q. What is the nickname given to the Connecticut River valley in northern Connecticut due to the major crop grown there?

A. Tobacco Valley.

Q. What group demanded improvement in the quality of Connecticut roads in the 1890s?

A. The League of American Wheelmen (a group of bicycle clubs).

Q. What is the official name for New Haven's Q Bridge?

A. Pearl Harbor Memorial Bridge.

Q. What is the only town in the state with land on both sides of the Connecticut River?

A. Haddam.

Q. What is the reason for the small "jog" in Connecticut's border with Massachusetts?

A. To correct for a surveyor's error.

Q. What is the size of Connecticut's smallest state forest, Topsmead?

A. 514 acres.

Q. What is the source of the name for the town of Avon, Connecticut?

A. The River Avon in England.

Q. The Connecticut River forms the boundary between what two states?

A. New Hampshire and Vermont.

Q. What is the state flower of Connecticut?

A. The mountain laurel.

Q. What town was by far the largest in Connecticut Colony, at over 225 square miles?

A. Farmington.

Q. What was the first name given to the settlement at present-day Wethersfield when it was settled in 1634?

A. Watertown.

Q. What is the state song of Connecticut?

A. "Yankee Doodle."

Q. What town is on Connecticut's southernmost border with New York?

A. Greenwich.

Q. What is the total number of state parks in Connecticut?

A. Fifty-seven.

Q. What is the vertical clearance under the Baldwin Bridge, which spans the Connecticut River near Long Island Sound?

A. Eighty-one feet.

Q. What Connecticut town was named for a doctor who promised the town a library in return for the honor but never lived up to his promise?

A. Sterling, named for Dr. John Sterling.

Q. What is the vertical drop of the waterfall at Kent Falls State Park?

A. Two hundred feet.

Q. What island, part of New York state, lies some three miles off the Connecticut coast south of Groton?

A. Fishers Island.

Q. What land can be seen from much of the Connecticut shoreline as one looks south?

A. Long Island, New York.

Q. What Litchfield County town has the distinction of being regarded as the coldest town in Connecticut?

A. Norfolk.

Q. What low mountain range passes through Connecticut's northwest corner?

A. The Taconic Mountains.

Q. What major western Massachusetts city is also served by Hartford's airport?

A. Springfield.

Q. What mountain summit is the highest in Connecticut?

A. Bear Mountain (2,316 feet).

Q. What name, descriptive of the color of East and West Rock, was given to the New Haven area by Dutch explorer Adriaen Block?

A. Rodeborg (red mountain).

Q. What natural barrier has prevented major industrial development along the Connecticut River?

A. A sandbar at the mouth of the river.

Q. What New Haven street is the center of the city's Italian neighborhood and home of several noted Italian restaurants?

A. Wooster.

Q. What longtime nickname did Willimantic have because of its association with the textile industry?

A. Thread City.

Q. What occupation ranks first in Connecticut, with the most people employed in that line of work?

A. Retail salespersons.

Q. The highest elevation in Connecticut is in what western county?

A. Litchfield.

Q. What is the highest place in Connecticut, although the peak is in Massachusetts?

A. Mount Frissell (2,380 feet).

Q. What river's mouth is at the southwestern border of Connecticut with New York?

A. The Byram.

Q. What Sicilian town is the ancestral home of many Italian-Americans now living in Middletown?

A. Melilli.

Q. What small group of islands lie off the Connecticut shoreline near Branford?

A. The Thimble Islands.

Q. What bridge spans the Thames River between New London and Groton?

A. Gold Star Memorial Bridge.

Q. What state nickname of Connecticut appears on some of its license plates?

A. The Constitution State.

Q. What term was given to the territory of Litchfield County when the land was being auctioned off as farmland in the early eighteenth century?

A. The Western Lands.

Q. What three Connecticut towns beginning with New were named after other towns in the state?

A. New Fairfield, New Hartford, and New Milford.

Q. What town is at Connecticut's extreme northwest corner?

A. Salisbury.

Q. What town is at the geographic center of Connecticut?

A. Berlin.

Q. What town is the most populous in Connecticut, with a population of 63,589 in 2000?

A. West Hartford.

🌳

Q. In 1996 what organization designated the Connecticut River estuary one of the "Last Great Places" in the Western Hemisphere?

A. The Nature Conservancy.

🌳

Q. What town's quarries yielded granite that was used to build the Brooklyn Bridge and the base of the Statue of Liberty?

A. Guilford.

🌳

Q. What towns contributed the first parts of their names to the town of Harwinton?

A. (Har)tford and (Win)dsor.

🌳

Q. What two digits do all Connecticut ZIP codes begin with?

A. 06.

🌳

Q. What percentage of Connecticut is forested land?

A. Approximately sixty.

🌳

Q. What two towns are at the mouth of the Connecticut River?

A. Old Saybrook and Old Lyme.

Q. What was an earlier name for the area now known as Cromwell?

A. Middletown Upper Houses.

Q. What was Connecticut's most populous town or city according to the 1800 Census?

A. Stonington (5,437).

Q. What was Cotton Mather's term for a Connecticut resident, recorded in 1702?

A. Connecticotian.

Q. What was Dutch explorer Adriaen Block's original name for the Connecticut River?

A. Versche (Fresh).

Q. What was the 1630s Dutch name for the area near present-day Saybrook Point?

A. Kievett's Hook (Dutch: Kievetts Hoek).

Q. What was the first town in Connecticut to be given a biblical name, in 1697?

A. Lebanon.

Q. What was the name (in English) of the 1633 Dutch colonial settlement at Hartford?

A. House of Good Hope.

Q. What Connecticut city has the state's largest public school enrollment?

A. Hartford (22,538 in 1999).

Q. Windham County was created in 1726 from land that had been part of what two original counties?

A. Hartford and New London.

Q. Litchfield County was created in 1751 from land that had been part of what two original counties?

A. Fairfield and Hartford.

Q. What was the epicenter of the May 16, 1791, earthquake, felt as far away as New York City and Boston?

A. East Haddam, near Moodus.

Q. When was the dispute over Connecticut's western boundary with New York, dating back to at least 1650, finally settled by the legislatures of both states and the U.S. Congress?

A. 1880.

Q. Middlefield's Lake Beseck derives its name from what Native American tribal name?

A. *Mattabeseck.*

Q. What is the name of the pond in Hartford's Elizabeth Park?

A. Lake Vista.

Q. Connecticut Avenue in Washington, D.C., is famous as the site of what?

A. Embassy Row, the street on which most foreign embassies are located.

Q. What Connecticut town ranked first in April 2001 on the list of America's most affluent communities?

A. Greenwich.

Q. In what year was Connecticut named "State of the Year" by the National Alliance of Business?

A. 2000.

Q. What was the 2001 ranking of the University of Connecticut among all public universities in New England?

A. First.

Q. What is said to be the Native American meaning of the name Connecticut?

A. Beside the long tidal river.

Q. What was the name of Granby prior to its establishment as a separate town in 1786?

A. Salmon Brook.

Q. What were the two staple crops cultivated by Native American inhabitants of Connecticut?

A. Corn and squash.

Q. Where was the mouth of the Connecticut River originally, in prehistoric times?

A. Near present-day New Haven.

🌳

Q. Which Connecticut city is largest in population?

A. Bridgeport (139,529 in the 2000 Census).

🌳

Q. What was one of the seventeenth-century names for the town of Newington?

A. Pipestave Swamp.

🌳

Q. Who is designated as Connecticut's state composer?

A. Charles Edward Ives.

🌳

Q. Who is the state hero of Connecticut?

A. Nathan Hale.

🌳

Q. What U.S. military academy is located in Connecticut?

A. The U.S. Coast Guard Academy, in New London.

🌳

Q. Windham County, in the northeast corner of Connecticut, is sometimes referred to by what nickname?

A. The Quiet Corner.

Q. What is Connecticut's rank among the fifty states in average annual income?

A. First.

Q. What is a common nickname for Interstate 91, from New Haven through Massachusetts?

A. The College Highway.

Q. Settled in 1633, what is Connecticut's oldest town?

A. Windsor.

ENTERTAINMENT

C H A P T E R   T W O

Q. In what town did comedienne and Academy Award–winning actress Whoopi Goldberg buy a colonial farmhouse in 1991?

A. Cornwall.

Q. How many people are estimated to have viewed Jumbo the Elephant of the Barnum & Bailey Circus in the 1880s?

A. Twenty million.

Q. How many productions first staged at New Haven's Shubert Performing Arts Center have gone on to Broadway?

A. Three hundred.

Q. A Shakespearean festival in what Connecticut town first impressed acting great Raymond Massey with the talents of fellow Canadian Christopher Plummer?

A. Stratford.

Q. How many slot machines are available at the Foxwoods Resort Casino?

A. Close to six thousand.

Q. Greenwich is home to what soul and pop music superstar, the lead singer of The Supremes?

A. Diana Ross.

Q. In what year did actor-director Jodie Foster, a 1985 Yale graduate, receive an honorary doctorate from her alma mater?

A. 1997.

Q. What summer-stock theater was one of the theatrical launching pads for Katharine Hepburn?

A. Ivoryton Playhouse.

Q. Adele Simpson, fashion designer to Hollywood stars and first ladies, made her home in what town?

A. Greenwich.

Q. At what New Haven nightclub did the Rolling Stones kick off their 1989 Steel Wheels tour?

A. Toad's Place.

Q. What Connecticut school includes Paul Newman and Jerry Seinfeld as graduates?

A. Skip Barber Racing School, Lime Rock Park.

Q. At what site can one purchase a CD of Gregorian chants performed by resident Benedictine nuns?

A. Abbey of Regina Laudis, Bethlehem.

Q. Buffalo Bill and sharpshooter Annie Oakley of the famed Wild West Shows used arms and ammunition from what New Haven manufacturer?

A. Winchester Repeating Arms Co.

Q. Enrico Caruso, William Gillette, and Ray Bolger performed at what western Connecticut playhouse?

A. Thomaston Opera House.

Q. How large is the screen of the IMAX theater at the Maritime Aquarium in Norwalk?

A. Eight stories wide by six stories high (80 feet by 60 feet).

Q. What is the name of the child care and entertainment center at Mohegan Sun?

A. Kids Quest.

Q. What 1975 movie starring Katharine Ross was set in a mythical Connecticut town?

A. *The Stepford Wives.*

Q. How many opera and light opera companies are located in Connecticut?

A. Nine.

Q. How many people died in the 1944 Ringling Brothers Circus tent fire in Hartford?

A. 168.

Q. What annual festival in southeastern Connecticut displays Native American music and dance from more than five hundred tribal nations?

A. Schemitzun.

Q. Engine No. 40 on the popular Essex Steam Train Ride was built in what year?

A. 1920.

Q. How many seats are there in the Bingo Hall at Foxwoods Resort Casino?

A. Thirty-two hundred.

Q. What are the only two Connecticut inns, among only thirty in the country, listed in the prestigious Relais & Chateaux directory of luxury accommodations?

A. Mayflower Inn (Washington) and the Inn at National Hall (Westport).

Q. What Bridgeport native played mailman "Cliff" in TV's *Cheers*?

A. John Ratzenberger.

Q. Forensics expert Dr. Henry C. Lee of Connecticut testified for the defense at the famous trial of what sports and media celebrity?

A. O. J. Simpson.

Q. What comedian, television star, and author is a regular headliner at the Foxwoods Casino theater?

A. Bill Cosby.

Q. *Quassy* in Quassy Amusement Park is actually short for what?

A. Lake Quassapaug.

Q. How old was P. T. Barnum when he started the Barnum & Bailey Circus?

A. Seventy-seven.

Q. In what Connecticut city was "There'll Be a Hot Time in the Old Town Tonight" first performed?

A. Waterbury.

Q. In what Connecticut towns is Paul Newman's charity Hole in the Wall Gang Camp?

A. Ashford and Eastford.

Q. In what movie, set in a fictional Connecticut country inn, did Bing Crosby introduce the song "White Christmas"?

A. Holiday Inn.

Q. In what New Haven cemetery is famed bandleader Glenn Miller honored with a cenotaph?

A. Grove Street Cemetery.

Q. In what year did Bridgeport-born Brian Dennehy win a Tony Award for his Broadway portrayal of Willy Loman in *Death of a Salesman?*

A. 1998.

🌳

Q. In what Connecticut town was famed showman Phineas T. Barnum born?

A. Bethel.

🌳

Q. In what year did Connecticut's second gambling casino, Mohegan Sun, open its doors?

A. 1996.

🌳

Q. James Brunot of Newtown invented what famous board game?

A. Scrabble.

🌳

Q. Lake Compounce Amusement Park set its all-time attendance record with a 1941 show starring what band and singer?

A. Tommy Dorsey Orchestra with Frank Sinatra.

🌳

Q. Redding Ridge-born Hope Lange made her screen debut in what film, which featured Marilyn Monroe?

A. *Bus Stop,* in 1956.

🌳

Q. Silent movie star Richard Barthelmess, whose film career began with D. W. Griffith's company, attended what Connecticut college?

A. Trinity College, Hartford.

Q. The country's only Museum of Fife and Drum is located in what Connecticut village?

A. Ivoryton.

Q. The Dairy Bar at the University of Connecticut, Storrs, enjoys a widespread reputation for the quality of what product made there?

A. Ice cream.

Q. The great Barnum & Bailey Circus fire of 1944, in Hartford, has been known as what?

A. "The Day the Clowns Cried."

Q. Television star Bob Crane, star of Hogan's Heroes, was from what Connecticut city?

A. Waterbury.

Q. What 1959 movie starring Doris Day and Jack Lemmon was filmed in Connecticut?

A. *It Happened to Jane.*

Q. In what twenty-one-state jackpot lottery does Connecticut participate?

A. Powerball.

Q. What Connecticut amusement park was the first family theme park in America?

A. Lake Compounce Amusement Park.

Q. In what year was the original run of the Valley Railroad, now used by the Essex Steam Train Ride?

A. 1871.

🌳

Q. What Connecticut venue has hosted top-name stars such as B. B. King, Reba McEntire, and TV comedian Ray Romano?

A. Uncas Pavilion at Mohegan Sun.

🌳

Q. What is the longest-running free jazz series in the country?

A. The Monday Night Jazz Series, Bushnell Park, Hartford.

🌳

Q. What Danbury summertime concert venue has featured Bob Dylan, Smokey Robinson, and The Moody Blues?

A. Charles Ives Center for the Arts.

🌳

Q. What Dave Brubeck CD, recorded in Stamford in 2000, features his solo piano music?

A. One Alone.

🌳

Q. What did Barnum's circus gross in its first year of operation, 1870?

A. $400,000.

🌳

Q. What English-born Killingworth resident wrote and illustrated the Dr. Doolittle stories, which became a children's and Hollywood favorite?

A. Hugh Lofting.

Q. What Essex-based company is a leading maker of traditional fifes and rope-tension drums used by fife and drum corporations worldwide?

A. Cooperman Fife & Drum Co.

Q. What exotic woods are used by Connecticut artisans for fife-making?

A. Cocobolo and grenadilla.

Q. What famed opera tenor has a home in Sharon, Connecticut?

A. Placido Domingo.

Q. What former CBS News reporter and commentator of *On the Road* fame lived in Essex?

A. Charles Kuralt.

Q. What former *Tonight Show* conductor founded a cooking school in New Milford?

A. Skitch Henderson.

Q. What gambling casino is located in Uncasville, Connecticut?

A. Mohegan Sun.

Q. What Grammy-winning popular ballad singer was born in New Haven?

A. Michael Bolton.

Q. What Grateful Dead songs did Bob Weir co-write with a Wesleyan alumnus?

A. "I Need a Miracle" and "Hell in a Bucket."

Q. What Hartford hotel proprietor sold the world's first bottled cocktails in 1892?

A. G. F. Heublein.

Q. What Hartford native starred in TV's *Big Valley* and *Dynasty*?

A. Linda Evans.

Q. What Hartford theatre company is the oldest continuous touring company in the United States?

A. National Theatre of the Deaf.

Q. What Hartford-made domestic product partly inspired two major motion pictures, in 1948 and 1950?

A. Fuller Brushes (*The Fuller Brush Man* and *The Fuller Brush Girl*).

Q. What is Connecticut's oldest continuously operating movie theater?

A. Bantam Cinema.

Q. What is featured at the "Haul of Fame" museum in Canterbury?

A. Antique trucks.

Q. What is New London's major performance venue, centered around a restored 1,530-seat 1926 theater?

A. Garde Arts Center.

Q. What is the admission fee at Old Lyme's Nut Museum?

A. One nut.

Q. What is the highest single play one can make on a slot machine at Mohegan Sun?

A. $500.

Q. In what year did the carousel in Hartford's Bushnell Park begin operation?

A. 1914.

Q. What Connecticut village is home to Whipple's Christmas Wonderland, featuring holiday displays with more than 100,000 lights?

A. Ballouville.

Q. What is the longest-running horror show and Halloween exhibit in America?

A. Witch's Dungeon Horror Museum, Bristol.

Q. What is the name of "The Nut Lady," founder and curator of Old Lyme's Nut Museum, featured on national TV?

A. Elizabeth Tashjian.

Q. What famed showman was once the mayor of Bridgeport?

A. P. T. Barnum.

Q. What famous African-American singer and actor hailed from Enfield, Connecticut?

A. Paul Robeson.

Q. What is the name of the circular movie theater at Foxwoods Casino?

A. Cinedrome 360.

Q. What is the name of the ghost that is said to haunt New London's Ledge Lighthouse?

A. Ernie.

Q. What is the name of the summer-stock theatrical company that produces shows at the Ivoryton Playhouse?

A. River Rep.

Q. What is the name of the water coaster ride at Quassy Amusement Park?

A. The Big Flush.

Q. What is the only agricultural fair in Connecticut that also incorporates a circus?

A. Guilford Fair.

Q. What is the overall deck length of the two-masted schooner *Mystic Whaler,* the reproduction out of Mystic harbor?

A. Eighty-three feet.

Q. What is the site of Norwalk's annual Oyster Festival?

A. Veteran's Memorial Park, East Norwalk.

Q. What is the special distinction of B. F. Clyde's Cider Mill in Mystic?

A. It is the last steam-powered cider mill in New England.

Q. What late-night television host makes his home in New Canaan?

A. David Letterman.

Q. What legendary singer supported herself in her teen years by farm and factory work in Connecticut?

A. Eartha Kitt.

Q. What macho Hollywood star of 125 feature films was born in Bridgeport?

A. Robert Mitchum.

Q. What member of the Rolling Stones calls Connecticut home?

A. Keith Richards.

Q. What musician, born in Connecticut, was a pioneer of the use of polytonality and polyrhythm in music?

A. Charles Ives.

Q. What Native American tribe operates the Foxwoods casino?

A. The Mashuntucket Pequot.

Q. What New Haven institution stages concerts for students and teachers and has an Instrument Petting Zoo on its site?

A. Neighborhood Music School.

Q. What Waterbury native introduced Russian-born ballet star Mikhail Baryshnikov to American audiences?

A. Lucia Chase.

Q. What New Haven native appeared in the movies *Josie and the Pussycats* and *Buffalo Soldiers*?

A. Gabriel Mann.

Q. What non-profit group sponsors concerts of Renaissance, Baroque, and other early musical styles at several New London–area venues?

A. Connecticut Early Music Society.

Q. What Norwalk dairy and grocery store is also known as an entertainment attraction for its live music and animated animal characters?

A. Stew Leonard's.

Q. What noted television cooking celebrity makes his home in Connecticut?

A. Jacques Pepin.

Q. What Oscar-nominated actress was born in Greenwich in 1947?

A. Glenn Close.

Q. In what year did Willimantic-born soprano Eileen Farrell debut at New York's Metropolitan Opera?

A. 1960.

Q. What Oscar-nominated and Emmy-winning actor was once an efficiency expert for the Connecticut state budget office?

A. Peter Falk.

Q. What Oscar-winning actress was born on Willow Street in Waterbury?

A. Rosalind Russell.

Q. What popular American composer and Woodbury resident wrote the Christmas favorite "Sleigh Ride."

A. Leroy Anderson.

Q. What popular radio show makes regular appearances on location at the Mohegan Sun casino?

A. *Imus in the Morning.*

Q. What private employer is the largest employer in the state of Connecticut?

A. Foxwoods Resort Casino.

Q. What promotional slogan did showman P. T. Barnum give to his circus?

A. The Greatest Show on Earth.

Q. What Prospect man became well known in the 1930s for his tall tales about a mythical farmer named Lester Green?

A. C. Louis Mortison.

Q. What role did Connecticut resident William Gillette make famous on the American stage?

A. Sherlock Holmes.

Q. What shoreline town once offered sightseeing rides aboard the *African Queen*, the original steamboat from the acclaimed movie?

A. Old Saybrook.

Q. What town annually hosts Connecticut's largest agricultural fair?

A. Durham.

Q. What Stamford-based market research company is known for its television ratings system?

A. A. C. Nielsen Corp.

Q. What star of the hit TV series *The X-Files* has a degree in English literature from Yale?

A. David Duchovny.

🌳

Q. What star of the TV show *ER* is a native of Hartford?

A. Eriq La Salle.

🌳

Q. What television soap opera once included a scene of the falls at Kent Falls State Park?

A. *Guiding Light.*

🌳

Q. What town annually hosts Connecticut's largest "muster," a parade of more than one hundred fife and drum corps?

A. Deep River.

🌳

Q. What singer in the Country Music Hall of Fame, who recorded the 1924 million-seller hit "The Prisoner's Song," lived his final years in Bridgeport?

A. Vernon Dalhart (Marion T. Slaughter).

🌳

Q. In what year did Yale University institute the Duke Ellington Fellowship to honor top jazz musicians?

A. 1972.

🌳

Q. What unique dish at Pat's Kountry Kitchen in Old Saybrook was invented after Pat's kids threw out the clam juice needed to make chowder?

A. Clam hash.

Q. What was the date of opening night for East Haddam's Goodspeed Opera House?

A. October 24, 1877.

Q. What was the first film in which Stamford-born film star Christopher Lloyd appeared?

A. *One Flew Over the Cuckoo's Nest,* in 1975.

Q. What was the first year of operation for Middlebury's Quassy Amusement Park?

A. 1908.

Q. What was the name of the man whom Barnum invited to join his circus as an equal partner in 1887?

A. James Bailey.

Q. What was the name used for the first American-made bicycles, built in Hartford?

A. Columbia.

Q. What was the actual name of famed circus midget "Tom Thumb"?

A. Charles Sherwood Stratton.

Q. What was the original name of the circus begun by Phineas T. Barnum?

A. P. T. Barnum's Grand Traveling Museum, Menagerie, Caravan, and Circus.

Q. What was the site of Connecticut's first Christmas tree, set up by a Hessian soldier in 1777?

A. Noden-Reed House, Windsor Locks.

Q. What Waterbury native founded the American Ballet Theatre in 1945?

A. Lucia Chase.

Q. Who was the star of the Mark Lamos production of *Hamlet* at the Hartford Stage?

A. Richard Thomas.

Q. What Wethersfield native was the author of the novel that was the basis for the TV movie *The Dark Secrets of Harvest Home*?

A. Thomas Tryon.

Q. What Winsted resident designed the monorail systems for both Disneyland and Disney World?

A. David Gengenbach.

Q. What world-famous candy is made in Orange, Connecticut?

A. PEZ.

Q. What world-renowned jazz artist from California has lived in Wilton since 1960?

A. Dave Brubeck.

Q. What Yale alumnus wrote two of Yale's fight songs, "Bull-Dog" and "Bingo, That's the Lingo"?

A. Cole Porter (Class of 1913).

Q. When did the Connecticut General Assembly establish the American Festival Shakespeare Theatre in Stratford?

A. June 1951.

Q. When Lake Compounce Amusement Park did not open in Spring 1993, it was the first spring it had not been open since what event?

A. The Civil War.

Q. Where are Connecticut's two trolley museums located?

A. East Haven and East Windsor.

Q. What was the peak year for drive-in theaters in Connecticut, with forty-two in operation?

A. 1967.

Q. Where are the two large outdoor shows called the Antiques Weekends held?

A. Farmington Polo Grounds.

Q. To what maximum height did P. T. Barnum's circus midget "Tom Thumb" grow?

A. Forty inches.

Q. Where did actor Roddy McDowall make his stage debut in Young Woodley?

A. Westport Country Playhouse.

Q. Where did actress Claire Danes, star of TV's *My So-called Life,* attend college?

A. Yale University.

Q. Where did operatic star Eileen Farrell of Willimantic show off her blues singing talent to rave reviews?

A. Spoleto Festival, 1959.

Q. Where does Academy Award–winning actor Dustin Hoffman have a country home?

A. Roxbury, Connecticut.

Q. Where in Connecticut can one see the Buck-A-Rama, with championship bull and bareback riding?

A. At the Schemitzun festival.

Q. Where is Connecticut's largest public shoreline park?

A. Hammonasset Beach State Park, Madison.

Q. Where is Connecticut's only jai alai fronton?

A. Milford.

Q. Where is the annual two-week Mum Festival, with a Mum Queen, a "mumathon" run, all at Mum City, U.S.A.?

A. Bristol.

Q. What Connecticut borough has long been the home of Katharine Hepburn?

A. Fenwick (part of Old Saybrook).

Q. Where is the Norma Terris Theatre, a smaller venue affiliated with the Goodspeed Opera House?

A. Chester.

Q. Where was Oscar-winning movie and TV star Ernest Borgnine born?

A. Hamden.

Q. Where was the Connecticut estate of two-time Oscar-winning actor Frederic March?

A. New Milford.

Q. Which now-deceased star of the original *Saturday Night Live* was a resident of Stamford?

A. Gilda Radner.

Q. Who directed the 1997 feature film *Amistad,* which documented the story of African slaves who were tried and released in Connecticut?

A. Steven Spielberg.

Q. Who invented the lollipop at the Bradley Smith Candy Co. of New Haven in 1892?

A. George C. Smith.

Q. What Connecticut city is home to the headquarters of the World Wrestling Federation?

A. Stamford.

Q. What Connecticut city is home to the National Shaving and Barbershop Museum?

A. Meriden.

Q. Who is the Fairfield man who invented the Wiffle Ball in 1954?

A. David N. Mullaney.

Q. What Connecticut College alumna starred with Rock Hudson in TV's *Macmillan and Wife*?

A. Susan St. James.

Q. What Connecticut company introduced the use of molded plastic to replace the use of ivory as a piano key covering?

A. Pratt, Read & Co.

Q. What Connecticut company manufactured the first Mickey Mouse watch?

A. Waterbury Clock Co.

Q. Who is the Hartford-born movie producer, journalist, and chronicler of Hollywood?

A. Dominick Dunne.

Q. Who is the Wesleyan University alumnus who co-wrote songs with Bob Weir of the Grateful Dead?

A. John Perry Barlow.

Q. What Connecticut gambling casino is said to be the largest in the Western hemisphere?

A. Foxwoods.

Q. What Connecticut historic museum has an original seven-hole outhouse on display?

A. Holley House Museum, Lakeville.

Q. What Connecticut radio station was the first in the world to broadcast in FM in 1939?

A. WDRC in Hartford.

Q. In what year was singer Pearl Bailey awarded a Duke Ellington Fellowship by Yale?

A. 1987.

Q. What Connecticut theater featured Orson Welles, Joseph Cotton, and others of the Mercury Players in the 1930s?

A. Stony Creek Puppet House Theatre.

Q. What Connecticut theater has been a testing ground for Broadway shows including *Annie* and *Man of La Mancha*?

A. The Goodspeed Opera House, East Haddam.

Q. Where was Vince McMahon, head of the World Wrestling Federation, born?

A. Greenwich.

Q. What Connecticut theater has on display a collection of antique Sicilian puppets?

A. Stony Creek Puppet House Theater.

Q. What Connecticut town annually hosts three agricultural fairs at its fairgrounds?

A. Goshen.

Q. What was the original name of the World Wrestling Federation?

A. Capitol Wrestling Corporation.

Q. Who starred in the 1957 movie *Fear Strikes Out*, which chronicled the life of Connecticut-born baseball player Jimmy Piersall?

A. Anthony Perkins.

Q. Who starred in the 1988 movie *Mystic Pizza,* about a small-town pizza parlor in Connecticut?

A. Julia Roberts.

Q. What Connecticut town hosts the annual Highland Festival, featuring Scottish food, music, and games?

A. Scotland.

Q. What Connecticut town is the home of Paul Newman and Joanne Woodward?

A. Westport.

Q. Who starred in the movie version of Mark Twain's *A Connecticut Yankee in King Arthur's Court?*

A. Bing Crosby.

Q. Who was the General Electric scientist who invented the material that came to be known as Silly Putty in a New Haven laboratory during World War II?

A. James Wright.

Q. What Connecticut town is the home of radio talk show host Don Imus?

A. Westport.

Q. What Connecticut train station, now a museum, appears in Alfred Hitchcock's 1951 film *Strangers on a Train?*

A. Danbury Union Station.

Q. Who was the Italian-born opera star who lived in Stamford and starred in Broadway's *South Pacific?*

A. Ezio Pinza.

Q. Who was the Middletown native who wrote patriotic songs for the Union cause in the Civil War, including "Marching Through Georgia"?

A. Henry Clay Work.

Q. Who was the noted entertainer who hosted the Greater Hartford Open for much of its history?

A. Sammy Davis Jr.

Q. Who was the real-life Connecticut murderess who inspired the author of *Arsenic and Old Lace*?

A. Amy Archer-Gilligan.

Q. Who was the Russian-born immigrant who came to Hartford and became a star of vaudeville as a singer and comedian?

A. Sophie Tucker.

Q. Who was the soprano, dubbed the "Swedish Nightingale," that P. T. Barnum introduced to American audiences in 1850?

A. Jenny Lind.

Q. Movie star Mel Gibson battled with what town wetlands agency about a sheep shed on his estate there?

A. Greenwich.

Q. Who won a Tony Award in 1989 for his artistic direction at the Hartford Stage Company?

A. Mark Lamos.

Q. Woodstock's Solair Recreation League is Connecticut's only facility offering what?

A. Nudist camping.

Q. How many drive-in theaters are still operating in Connecticut?

A. Three.

Q. What Emmy and Golden Globe-winning actress, who appeared in TV's *Lou Grant* and *The Sopranos*, is buried in an unknown cemetery in Connecticut?

A. Nancy Marchand.

Q. What Canadian-born actor, star of the 1940 movie *Abe Lincoln in Illinois*, is buried in Eastford, Connecticut?

A. Raymond Massey.

Q. Comedian Al Schacht, who was the original "Clown Prince of Baseball," is buried in what Connecticut town?

A. Woodbury.

HISTORY

Q. What New Haven eatery is said to be the place where America's first pizza was served?

A. Pepe's Pizza.

Q. Hartford is best known as a major center for what industry?

A. Insurance.

Q. Who christened the *Columbia,* the last Los Angeles–class submarine built in Groton, in 1994?

A. First Lady Hillary Rodham Clinton.

Q. In what year is the Griswold Inn of Essex said to have first opened for business?

A. 1776.

Q. The town of Scotland was named in 1700 by what Scottish immigrant?

A. Isaac Magune.

Q. What native of Sherman was a founder of Ohio's Oberlin College in 1833?

A. Philo Penfield Stewart.

Q. The First Company Governor's Horse Guard has what distinction in American military history?

A. It is the oldest cavalry unit still active.

Q. In what town was Charles Lewis Tiffany, founder of New York's Tiffany & Company, born?

A. Killingly.

Q. In what year was Connecticut's first state house built in Hartford?

A. 1720.

Q. In what year was Connecticut's original newspaper begun?

A. 1755 (*Connecticut Gazette* in New Haven).

Q. In what year did Mary Hall of Marlborough become the first woman admitted to the Connecticut Bar Association?

A. 1882.

Q. What New Haven mayor was the only man to sign all four of America's founding documents?

A. Roger Sherman (Articles of Association, Declaration of Independence, Articles of Confederation, and the U.S. Constitution).

Q. In what Connecticut city did the trial of the Amistad mutineers take place?

A. New Haven.

Q. What Connecticut village was once the center for the manufacturing of ivory goods?

A. Ivoryton.

Q. What Connecticut town was a major center for the manufacture of piano actions?

A. Deep River.

Q. What was the original religious affiliation of Wesleyan University?

A. Methodist.

Q. What first name was the most popular for girls born in Connecticut in 1998?

A. Emily.

Q. What first name was the most popular for boys born in Connecticut in 1998?

A. Michael.

Q. King Philip's War, which ended Native American resistance in Connecticut, ended in what year?

A. 1676.

Q. What Congregational minister led his followers to the site of Hartford and helped found the city?

A. Thomas Hooker.

Q. When was Connecticut's colonial charter replaced by a more modern constitution?

A. 1818.

Q. For what is Gen. Moses Cleaveland, who was born and died in Canterbury, best known?

A. Founding the city of Cleveland, Ohio.

Q. In what year did the Chester-Hadlyme ferry begin operation?

A. 1769.

Q. Rev. Eleazer Wheelock, founder of Dartmouth College, started his first school in what Connecticut town?

A. Lebanon (later Columbia).

Q. What town is the birthplace of Commodore Isaac Hull, commander of the USS *Constitution* (Old Ironsides)?

A. Derby.

Q. Women from what town submitted the first anti-slavery petition to the U.S. Congress in 1840?

A. Glastonbury.

Q. What central Ohio city was founded by citizens of Granby, Connecticut?

A. Worthington.

Q. What noted museum of Native American culture is found in Uncasville?

A. Tantaquidgeon Indian Museum.

Q. President William Howard Taft resided in what residence hall while attending Yale?

A. Connecticut Hall.

Q. What leather-like upholstery material was developed in Naugatuck, Connecticut?

A. Naugahyde.

Q. Abraham Ribicoff, who served in both houses of Congress, as governor of Connecticut, and as Secretary of Health, Education, and Welfare, was born in what city?

A. New Britain.

Q. In what year was the Spanish bell in St. Stephen's Church in East Haddam cast?

A. A.D. 815.

Q. A resident of Windsor, who was the first person to be executed for witchcraft in America?

A. Alice Young.

Q. Among the thirteen original states, in what order did Connecticut rank in ratification of the U.S. Constitution?

A. Fifth.

Q. In what year did Connecticut's Charter Oak fall victim to a violent wind storm?

A. 1856.

Q. In what year did Hartford's Pope Manufacturing build the country's first motorcycle?

A. 1903.

Q. Aside from Silas Deane and Roger Sherman, who else represented Connecticut at the First Continental Congress in 1774?

A. Eliphalet Dyer.

Q. At Natchaug State Forest in Eastford can be found the ruins of the birthplace of what Union general, the first to be killed in the Civil War?

A. Gen. Nathaniel Lyon.

Q. At the start of the Civil War, Connecticut led the nation in railroad density with how many miles of track?

A. 601 miles.

Q. What Connecticut town was the birthplace of Little Sorrel, the favorite horse of Confederate Gen. Stonewall Jackson?

A. Somers, at Collins Farm.

Q. In what year did Yale graduate Eli Whitney invent the cotton gin?

A. 1794.

Q. In what year was the first U.S.-made cigar rolled, in East Windsor?

A. 1801.

Q. At what building in Wethersfield did George Washington and Rochambeau confer in 1781?

A. Webb House.

Q. Connecticut's first two cities, incorporated in January 1784, were New Haven and what other?

A. New London.

Q. Connecticut's four original counties in 1666 were Hartford, New Haven, Fairfield, and what other?

A. New London County.

Q. Connecticut's Freedom Trail, featuring more than sixty historic sites, documents what nineteenth-century movement?

A. The abolition of slavery.

Q. Elias Howe invented the first lock-stitch sewing machine in 1846 while he was living where?

A. The New Hartford Hotel.

Q. In what year was the Golden Hill Reservation of the Paugussett Native American tribe established in Trumbull?

A. 1659.

Q. In what year was the Housatonic Railroad begun, running from Bridgeport to Massachusetts?

A. 1837.

Q. Groton's National Submarine Wall of Honor is dedicated to what?

A. The fifty-two U.S. submarines lost in World War II.

Q. How many Twin Wasp airplane engines were produced by East Hartford's Pratt & Whitney?

A. 173,618, more than any other engine type in history.

Q. About how many years of documentary history are deposited at the Museum of Connecticut History?

A. 350.

Q. In 1791 President George Washington named Connecticut native David Humphreys the first United States Minister to what country?

A. Portugal.

Q. In what year was the current constitution of Connecticut enacted?

A. 1965.

Q. In 1810 the country's first cigar factory opened in what Connecticut town?

A. Suffield.

Q. In his early years Eli Whitney was the country's sole maker of what product?

A. Ladies' hatpins.

Q. What city is home to the northeast's first police museum, documenting nearly 150 years of that city's police force?

A. Hartford.

Q. In what Hartford neighborhood was the Pope Manufacturing Co., the American bicycle and motorcycle pioneer?

A. Frog Hollow.

Q. In what town is Connecticut's Valley Forge, where Gen. Israel Putnam encamped with his troops during the hard winter of 1778–79?

A. Redding.

Q. In what year did Connecticut pass the country's first aeronautical law to ensure public safety?

A. 1911.

Q. In what year did Connecticut raise its maximum speed limit to 65 MPH, the last state in the continental United States to do so?

A. 1998.

Q. How many citizens of Hartford served in the military in the Civil War?

A. Four thousand.

Q. How many Connecticut representatives signed the Declaration of Independence?

A. Four.

Q. In what year did the Robert Mill's Custom House in New London begin operation?

A. 1833.

Q. In what year was the founding of Yale University authorized by the Connecticut General Assembly?

A. 1701.

Q. How many public ferries operated on the Connecticut River in 1750?

A. Twenty-six.

Q. In what year were Connecticut's final two counties, Middlesex and Tolland, formed?

A. 1785.

Q. How many separate towns were created from the land that was originally part of Farmington?

A. Seven.

Q. In what year were the first King's Highways so designated in Connecticut?

A. 1679.

Q. In what years did Connecticut native J. Pierpont Morgan prevent national financial disasters by helping to fund the U.S. Treasury?

A. 1895 and 1907.

Q. Madison resident Cornelius Bushnell was one of the founders of what major railroad?

A. Union Pacific Railway.

Q. Middlefield's Lyman Orchards has been in the same family for how many generations?

A. Eight.

Q. On what date did East Hartford–based Pratt & Whitney finish its first airplane engine, the Wasp?

A. Christmas Eve 1925.

Q. On what date did English Puritans sail into what became known as New Haven harbor?

A. April 24, 1638.

Q. In what year did John Mason lead colonists in the Pequot War?

A. 1637.

Q. In what year did New York and Connecticut settle their boundary dispute, resulting in the "panhandle" at the southwest corner of the state?

A. 1683.

Q. On what date did the Mianus River Bridge over Interstate 95 in Greenwich collapse?

A. June 28, 1983.

Q. In what year was Connecticut's royal charter hidden in the Charter Oak to keep it from the agent of King James II?

A. 1687.

Q. In what year was Essex honored as the Best Small Town in America?

A. 1996.

Q. On what date was Connecticut officially admitted into the Union?

A. January 9, 1788.

Q. On what date was Hartford's Soldiers and Sailors Memorial Arch dedicated?

A. September 17, 1886.

Q. Prior to being converted to a prison in 1773, what was the site of Old Newgate Prison used for?

A. A copper mine.

Q. Radio station WDRC in Hartford was first located in what city?

A. New Haven.

Q. On what date was the first practical flight of a helicopter in the Western Hemisphere, piloted by Igor Sikorsky in Stratford?

A. September 14, 1939.

Q. On whose property was the Charter Oak located when it was used to hide the royal charter?

A. Samuel Wyllys.

Q. Rev. Thomas Hooker's congregation moved to the Hartford area from what place in Massachusetts?

A. Cambridge (then called Newtown).

Q. When were the tolls finally removed from Route 15, the Merritt Parkway–Wilbur Cross Parkway combination?

A. June 1988.

Q. Revolutionary War hero Ethan Allen was born in what Connecticut town?

A. Litchfield.

Q. What Connecticut native devised the U.S. Constitution's Connecticut Compromise, which established different bases of representation in the U.S. House and Senate?

A. Roger Sherman.

Q. The 1,200-foot long tunnel on the Wilbur Cross Parkway passes through what ridge?

A. West Rock.

Q. The Charter Oak stood at the corner of what present Hartford streets?

A. Charter Oak Place and Charter Oak Avenue.

Q. The Henry Whitfield House and Museum in Guilford was built in what year?

A. 1639.

Q. On what date was the last toll booth on any bridge or highway in Connecticut removed?

A. April 28, 1989 (on the Charter Oak Bridge).

Q. The Mohegan Road, later Route 32 between Norwich and New London, was laid out in what year?

A. 1670.

Q. The Native American chief called Metacom, whose warriors attacked Simsbury in 1676, was also known as what?

A. King Philip.

Q. The New Haven eatery Louis' Lunch is said to have been the first ever to serve what?

A. The hamburger (in 1895).

Q. The Nipmunk Native American tribe of northeast Connecticut was also known by what name?

A. Wabbaquassetts.

Q. The tall ship used for training by the U.S. Coast Guard in New London is named what?

A. USS *Eagle*.

Q. What 1639 document, written in Hartford, is considered the first written constitution for a democracy?

A. The Fundamental Orders of 1639.

Q. For what are Connecticut industrialists Walter H. Bowes and Arthur Pitney best known?

A. Marketing the first postage meter, 1920.

Q. What Canton-based company was once the largest edge-tool manufacturer in the world?

A. Collins Axe Company.

Q. What center of abolitionist activity has been called the Grand Central Station of Connecticut's pre–Civil War Underground Railroad?

A. Farmington.

Q. What city has a memorial to the Mohegan chief Uncas at its Indian Burial Ground?

A. Norwich.

Q. What company in Windsor Locks developed the first tea bag and the first packaged sheet toilet paper?

A. Dexter Corp.

Q. What Connecticut city once produced half of all the silverware in the United States?

A. Meriden.

Q. In what year was slavery abolished in Connecticut?

A. 1848.

Q. The New London–based USS *Eagle* is what type of ship?

A. A barque.

Q. In what year was the first steamboat voyage up the Connecticut River?

A. 1815.

Q. What Connecticut city was once the center of the hat industry?

A. Danbury.

Q. What Connecticut city was the first to have regular steamboat service in 1815?

A. New Haven.

Q. On what date did the new Baldwin Bridge open, replacing the 1948 span?

A. May 25, 1993.

Q. On what date did the roof of the Hartford Civic Center collapse?

A. January 17, 1978.

Q. What Connecticut entrepreneur sold his products from a buggy in the 1840s, and eventually started a major tool manufacturing company?

A. Frederick T. Stanley.

Q. In what year did Samuel Colt of Hartford patent the first working revolver?

A. 1835.

Q. What Connecticut governor was able to secure a royal charter for the colony in 1661–62?

A. John Winthrop Jr.

Q. In what year did the Connecticut Legislature authorize a lottery to pay for road construction?

A. 1793.

Q. In what year did the iron smelter called the Kent Furnace begin operation?

A. 1826.

Q. What Connecticut governor approved the construction of the Connecticut Turnpike (now I-95 and I-395)?

A. John Davis Lodge.

Q. What Connecticut governor had the longest term of office?

A. Gurdon Saltonstall (1708–24).

Q. What Connecticut governor was the only colonial governor to support American independence?

A. Jonathan Trumbull.

Q. What Connecticut museum has the largest display of American production clocks?

A. American Clock and Watch Museum, Bristol.

Q. What Connecticut highway features one hundred evergreen trees in its median as a memorial to the state residents who died in the battle for Iwo Jima?

A. Route 9 between I-84 and Route 72 (Iwo Jima Highway).

Q. What Connecticut resident said, "Don't fire until you see the whites of their eyes," at the 1775 Battle of Bunker Hill (Breed's Hill)?

A. Gen. Israel Putnam.

Q. What Connecticut town hosts an annual "Blessing of the Fleet" for its commercial fishing fleet?

A. Stonington.

Q. What Connecticut town hosts an annual Blessing of the Motorcycles?

A. Litchfield, at Lourdes Shrine.

Q. What Connecticut museum is dedicated to the Victorian era and features guides in Victorian dress?

A. Hicks-Stearns House Museum, Tolland.

Q. What Connecticut governor was the first woman to be elected a state governor in her own right?

A. Ella T. Grasso.

Q. What Connecticut town was the birthplace of famed abolitionist John Brown?

A. Torrington.

Q. What Derby native served as an aide to Generals Putnam, Greene, and Washington in the Revolutionary War?

A. David Humphreys.

Q. What did Hartford inventor William Gray install at the Hartford Bank in 1889?

A. The first coin-operated telephone in the world.

Q. What did Oliver Winchester manufacture at his New Haven factory prior to the legendary Winchester repeating rifle?

A. Men's shirts.

Q. What English king granted the Connecticut Colony a royal charter in 1662?

A. Charles II.

Q. What Connecticut town was the birthplace of pioneer Moses Austin, whose plan for a Texas colony was carried out by his son, Stephen?

A. Durham.

Q. In what year did the first execution for witchcraft in New England take place in Windsor?

A. 1647.

Q. What French general marched across Connecticut in 1781 and camped in several places on his way to joining Washington's forces at Yorktown?

A. Rochambeau.

Q. What two Connecticut towns operated official post offices in 1746?

A. New London and Stonington.

Q. What Hartford building features a blue onion-shaped dome with a rampant horse atop?

A. The Colt Firearms factory.

Q. What is the name of the two historic houses in New London that are now a museum?

A. Hempsted Houses.

Q. What is the name of the vast coin and medal collection now stored at the Connecticut State Library?

A. The Mitchelson Coin Collection (named for its benefactor).

Q. What is the national distinction of the Old State House in Hartford?

A. It is the oldest extant state house in America.

Q. What Hartford woman fought for women's rights and suffrage through the latter half of the 1800s along with Susan B. Anthony and Elizabeth Cady Stanton?

A. Isabella Beecher Hooker.

Q. What Hartford-born financier and industrialist helped organize both the New York Central Railroad and United States Steel?

A. J. Pierpont Morgan.

Q. What is by far the oldest lock on display at Terryville's Lock Museum of America?

A. A four-thousand-year-old Egyptian lock.

Q. What is featured on the town seal of Windham, Connecticut?

A. A frog.

Q. What is the 1751 house, home of the Kent Historical Society, that is on the National Register of Historic Places?

A. Seven Hearths.

Q. What is the date on the oldest gravestone in Connecticut, that of Rev. Ephraim Huit of Windsor?

A. 1644.

Q. What was the time it took the mail stagecoach to travel from Norwich to Hartford in 1845?

A. Six and one-half hours.

Q. What Hartford building is said to be the first two-sided building in the world?

A. The Phoenix Mutual Insurance building or "boat building" (with two arcing sides).

Q. What Hartford company printed the first U.S. commemorative stamp, commemorating the U.S. centenary in 1876?

A. Plimpton Manufacturing Co.

Q. When was Connecticut and New England's first turnpike opened, between New London and Norwich?

A. 1792.

Q. When was the first railroad between New Haven and Hartford completed?

A. 1838.

Q. What is the official name of the historical society in the shoreline town of Guilford?

A. The Guilford Keeping Society.

Q. What is the oldest surviving American aircraft artifact, displayed at the New England Air Museum in Windsor Locks?

A. A balloon basket from the 1870s.

Q. In what year did the Hartford & New Haven Railroad line open, linking the (then) two state capitals?

A. 1839.

Q. In what year did the insurance business begin in Hartford, with a policy issued by Hartford Fire Insurance Co.?

A. 1794.

Q. What Madison resident was the chief financier of the Civil War ironclad ship the USS *Monitor*?

A. Cornelius Bushnell.

Q. What material were the first coins minted in the Connecticut colony made of?

A. Copper.

Q. What museum boasts the largest collection of locks, keys, and Victorian hardware in America?

A. Lock Museum of America, Terryville.

Q. What New Haven prep school, founded in 1660, is the fifth oldest educational institution in the country?

A. Hopkins School.

Q. What New Haven streets are named for three of the English regicides who participated in the trial and execution of King Charles I?

A. Whalley Avenue, Dixwell Avenue, and Goffe Street.

Q. What New London historic site was the headquarters of Connecticut's naval office during the Revolutionary War?

A. Shaw-Perkins Mansion.

Q. What nickname for New London reflects its major nineteenth-century industry?

A. The Whaling City.

Q. What noted American Revolutionary War figure was born in Norwich in 1841?

A. Benedict Arnold.

Q. What number is displayed on the conning tower of the USS *Nautilus,* built in Groton?

A. 571.

Q. What one-time Connecticut governor also served in Congress and as ambassador to India?

A. Chester Bowles.

Q. Where was the first Girls Club in the United States opened in 1864?

A. Waterbury.

Q. Where was the last encampment of the French army in Connecticut as it marched to Boston after the Revolutionary War's Battle of Yorktown?

A. Voluntown.

Q. What post rider from East Windsor announced the start of the Revolutionary War in Connecticut?

A. Israel Bissell.

Q. What product, invented in Stamford, revolutionized the use of hair coloring?

A. Miss Clairol Hair Color Bath.

Q. Where did the first ferry across the Connecticut River operate in 1641?

A. Windsor.

Q. What Revolutionary War patriot and martyr was born in Coventry, Connecticut?

A. Nathan Hale.

Q. What Simsbury company dominated the market for metered gasoline pumps through the 1960s, with a market share of 90 percent?

A. Veeder-Root Inc.

Q. What Stamford resident invented revolving type (later used by the IBM Selectric) for typewriters in the 1890s?

A. George C. Blickensderfer.

Q. What Stamford resident patented the first electric shaver in 1828?

A. Col. Jacob Schick.

Q. What street in East Hartford is named for the fact that a French army paid its troops there during their 1781 encampment?

A. Silver Lane.

Q. What town annually hosts a Victory over Japan parade on August 14?

A. Moosup.

Q. Where was the original Colt revolver manufactured in 1836?

A. Paterson, New Jersey.

Q. What two Connecticut natives directed the 1775 attack on Fort Ticonderoga, the first Crown property to fall in the Revolutionary War?

A. Ethan Allen and Benedict Arnold.

Q. What Groton-born Yale alumnus was sent to France in 1776 and convinced the French to side with the American Revolutionary cause?

A. Silas Deane.

Q. What two U.S. vice presidents were graduates of the Tapping Reeve Law School in Litchfield?

A. Aaron Burr and John C. Calhoun.

Q. What U.S. senator from Connecticut was the first vice presidential candidate of the Jewish faith?

A. Joseph Lieberman.

🌳

Q. What was George Washington's nickname for Connecticut during the Revolutionary War, for the supplies it provided?

A. The Provision State.

🌳

Q. What was the Connecticut vote for accepting the Federal Constitution of 1788?

A. 128–40.

🌳

Q. What was the first factory to be lit by electric light in 1878?

A. Willimantic Linen Co.

🌳

Q. What was the full name of Groton-born Mother Bailey, who assisted American soldiers in the Revolutionary War and War of 1812?

A. Anna Warner Bailey.

🌳

Q. Where was assembly-line manufacturing first used in 1809?

A. Brewster's Carriage Factory, New Haven.

🌳

Q. What was the original meaning of the call letters of WDRC, Connecticut's first commercial radio station?

A. D(oolittle)-R(adio)-C(orporation), for Franklin M. Doolittle, pioneer of Connecticut radio.

Q. What was the top speed limit in Connecticut's (and America's) first automobile speed limit law in 1900?

A. Twelve miles per hour.

Q. What was the Vermont militia formed by Connecticut-born Ethan Allen to enforce local property rights?

A. The Green Mountain Boys.

Q. What was the original name of Yale University when it was founded?

A. The Collegiate School.

Q. How many hours did it take for the 1815 stagecoach to travel from New Haven to New York City?

A. Fifteen.

Q. What is the name of the spot in Salisbury where iron ore deposits were discovered, prompting the development of iron smelting in the 1700s?

A. Ore Hill.

Q. What was the title used for the head of a Native American tribe in Connecticut?

A. Sachem ("SAY-chem").

Q. What was the village of Riverton once called, reflective of its chief industry in the 1800s?

A. Hitchcocksville (for the Hitchcock Chair Co.).

Q. What was the original name of the University of Connecticut?

A. Storrs Agricultural College.

Q. Where was the ceremony at which President Jimmy Carter formally presented the decommissioned USS *Nautilus* to the state of Connecticut?

A. Hartford's Old State House.

Q. Where was the first American Bishop of the Episcopal Church elected in 1783?

A. Woodbury, at Glebe House.

Q. What town is home to the Military Historians Museum, boasting one of the largest collections of military uniforms in the country?

A. Westbrook.

Q. Where was the site of the first Borden's condensed milk factory, opened in 1857?

A. Burr Pond, Torrington.

Q. What was the world's largest toy manufacturer in 1941, based in New Haven?

A. A. C. Gilbert Co. (maker of Erector Sets).

Q. What were the original call letters of Connecticut's first commercial radio station, in 1922?

A. WPAJ, New Haven.

Q. What were the years of operation of the Saybrook-Lyme ferry on the Connecticut River?

A. 1662–1911.

Q. Where was America's first carpet factory established in 1825?

A. Tarriffville, in Simsbury.

Q. When did Connecticut's current state capitol building first open for legislative business?

A. January 1879.

Q. When was the Woodstock Theft Detecting Society, one of the nation's oldest law-enforcement organizations, founded?

A. May 20, 1783.

Q. When were the last tolls removed from Interstate 95 (formerly the Connecticut Turnpike)?

A. October 1985.

Q. Where did the Amistad mutineers live while awaiting their return to Africa?

A. Farmington.

Q. What Revolutionary War patriot established Connecticut's first paper mill, and also manufactured woolen cloth, stockings, and chocolates?

A. Christopher Leffingwell of Norwich.

Q. Where is the 1826 barn, the last one left in New England built of brick?

A. Windsor Locks.

Q. Where is the Colt's Patent Firearms Manufacturing Company Factory Collection now on display?

A. The Museum of Connecticut History, Hartford.

Q. Where is the Nathan Hale Schoolhouse, where the Revolutionary War patriot once taught?

A. East Haddam.

Q. Where is the oldest still-operating railroad depot in the country, built in 1872?

A. Canaan.

Q. Where is Thomas Hooker, founder of Hartford and author of the Fundamental Orders of 1639, buried?

A. The Ancient Burial Ground, Hartford.

Q. Who was the first European to visit Connecticut?

A. Dutch explorer Adriaen Block.

Q. What was the nickname of the railroad that linked New York and Boston, which ran the high-speed white Ghost Train through Connecticut?

A. The Airline.

Q. What was the name of Pres. George H. W. Bush's father, one-time U.S. Senator from Connecticut?

A. Prescott Sheldon Bush.

Q. What was the name of the ornate mansion built by Samuel Colt in Hartford?

A. Armsmear.

Q. What was the name of Windsor's original stockaded settlement, built in the 1630s?

A. The Palisado.

Q. Where was Connecticut's bloodiest battle of the Revolutionary War, in 1781?

A. Fort Griswold, New London.

Q. Where was the 1783 meeting that established the Protestant Episcopal Church in the United States?

A. Glebe House in Woodbury.

Q. Who built the iron smelter in Furnace Village, the former name of present-day Lakeville?

A. Ethan Allen.

Q. Who donated money to found the Sloane-Stanley Museum in Kent, which displays early farming implements?

A. Stanley Works.

Q. Who established the first law school in the United States at Litchfield in 1784?

A. Tapping Reeve.

Q. Who established The Stamford Foundry Co., the nation's first cast-iron stove foundry, in 1830?

A. George E. Waring.

Q. Who first manufactured witch hazel in Essex, and gave birth to the company that later became the world-famous Dickinson Company?

A. Alvan Whittemore and Charles Champlin.

Q. Who gave the baccalaureate sermon at Wesleyan University in 1964?

A. Rev. Martin Luther King Jr.

Q. Who is the Native American chief buried in the Ponset section of Haddam?

A. Cockaponset.

Q. Who manufactured the first machine-made horseshoe nails in Hartford in 1866?

A. George Capewell.

Q. Who started a brush-making factory in Hartford that grew into a famous global business?

A. Alfred C. Fuller (Fuller Brush Co.).

Q. Who started the newspaper called *Connecticut Courant* (now called the *Hartford Courant*) in 1764?

A. Thomas Green.

Q. Who strongly promoted the Good Roads Movement for the pavement of American roads?

A. Hartford bicycle and car manufacturer Albert Pope.

Q. Who was appointed as the first United States National Commissioner of Education in 1867?

A. Dr. Henry Barnard of Hartford.

Q. Who was the African-American soldier who fought in the Civil War on the USS *Monitor* and is buried in Putnam?

A. Thomas L. Taylor.

Q. Who was the agent of King James II who tried to seize Connecticut's royal charter?

A. Sir Edmund Andros.

Q. Who was the Danbury girl who rode through New York's Putnam County in 1777 warning that the British were burning Danbury?

A. Sybil Ludington (at age sixteen).

Q. Who was the first Chinese immigrant to receive an American college degree, at Yale in 1854?

A. Yung Wing.

Q. Who were Connecticut's first two U.S. Senators?

A. Oliver Ellsworth and William Samuel Johnson.

Q. Who was the first large benefactor of the Collegiate School, for whom its name was changed?

A. Elihu Yale.

Q. Who was the first U.S. president to ride in a car, an electric-powered Pope built in Hartford, on August 22, 1902?

A. Theodore Roosevelt.

Q. Who was the Norwich-born turncoat who helped plan and lead the 1781 British attack on Fort Griswold?

A. Benedict Arnold.

Q. Who was the pilot of the first American dirigible flight, in Hartford in 1878?

A. Mark Quinlan.

Q. Who was the priest who founded the Knights of Columbus in New Haven in 1882?

A. Fr. Michael J. McGivney.

Q. Who was the Torrington-born financier who helped found the Central Pacific Railroad and was president of the Southern Pacific?

A. Collis Potter Huntington.

Q. Who was the Windsor-born preacher who led the 1740s Great Awakening movement in the Congregational Church?

A. Jonathan Edwards.

Q. What Windsor native was on the committee of five to draft the Constitution and later served as Chief Justice of the Supreme Court?

A. Oliver Ellsworth.

Q. Whose company manufactured the first Colt-designed revolvers in Connecticut in 1847, under contract to Samuel Colt?

A. Eli Whitney Jr.

Q. With a total length of eighty-six miles, what was the longest canal ever built in New England?

A. Farmington Canal.

Q. Who ran Connecticut's colonial mint, which made copper coins in Simsbury (now a part of East Granby) in the 1730s?

A. Samuel Higley.

Q. What statement, in a sermon by Rev. Thomas Hooker, was the basis for the autonomy asserted in Connecticut's first constitution, the Fundamental Orders of 1638?

A. "The foundation of authority is laid in the free consent of the people."

Q. In the 1662 Charter of the Colony of Connecticut, what is the full name given to the colony?

A. "Governour and Company of the English Collony of Connecticut in New England in America."

Q. On what date and in what place did King Charles II sign the Charter of the Colony of Connecticut?

A. April 23, 1662, at Westminster (now part of London, England).

Q. What was the name of Connecticut's first governor, in 1639?

A. John Haynes.

Q. How many of Connecticut's governors have had the family name Trumbull?

A. Four (Jonathan; Jonathan Jr.; Joseph; John H.)

Q. What was the original colonial name of the town that is now called Windsor?

A. Dorchester.

Q. What was the cost of a gallon of rum in 1839 at George Kimberly's General Store in the Westville section of New Haven?

A. Eighty-one cents.

Q. In what New Haven cemetery can one find the grave of lexicographer Noah Webster?

A. Grove Street Cemetery.

Q. What is the name of the farm museum in Guilford that was owned by the same family for 350 years and in 1991 was willed to a nonprofit foundation?

A. Dudley Farm.

Q. What Connecticut town is the home of the New England Civil War Museum?

A. Vernon.

Q. What is the image on the "tails" side of the new state quarter for Connecticut?

A. The charter oak.

Q. Where was the country's first planned "factory town" established in 1806?

A. Seymour.

ARTS & LITERATURE

C H A P T E R   F O U R

Q. Alexander Calder, who lived for a time in Roxbury, is most closely associated with what type of abstract sculpture?

A. The mobile.

Q. Connecticut native Frederick Law Olmsted is considered the American "father" of what artistic specialty?

A. Landscape architecture.

Q. Connecticut's royal charter is displayed at the State Library in a frame made of what?

A. Oak cut from the Charter Oak tree.

Q. Cyrus Northrup of Ridgefield was president of what university from 1884 to 1911?

A. University of Minnesota.

Q. During what years did Mark Twain actually reside in Hartford?

A. 1874–91.

Q. How many entries are in Noah Webster's 1828 magnum opus, *An American Dictionary of the English Language*?

A. Seventy thousand.

🌳

Q. Educational reformer Dr. Henry Barnard of Hartford was president of what two institutions?

A. University of Wisconsin (1859–61) and St. John's College, Maryland (1866–67).

🌳

Q. Famed landscape designer Frederick Law Olmsted designed what park in New Britain?

A. Walnut Hill Park.

🌳

Q. What book compiled by West Hartford–born Noah Webster was the most popular American book in the nineteenth century?

A. The so-called Blue-backed Speller (*A Grammatical Institute of the English Language*).

🌳

Q. What book is said to be the first biography of an American that was written by an American?

A. *Life of Israel Putnam* by David Humphrey (1788).

🌳

Q. What Connecticut artist has been called "The Audubon of the Fishing World"?

A. James Prosek (*Trout: An Illustrated History*).

🌳

Q. In what year did a Hartford publisher issue the first children's magazine in America?

A. 1789.

Q. Grace Moore, the noted opera star and actress of the 1930s, was a resident of what town?

A. Newtown.

🌳

Q. How many of Yale-educated James Fenimore Cooper's novels feature his most famous character Natty Bumppo?

A. Five.

🌳

Q. What Connecticut artist lives in a house made of hay bales (the Hay House) in Old Saybrook?

A. David Brown.

🌳

Q. What Connecticut church is said to be the most photographed in the state?

A. Litchfield Congregational Church.

🌳

Q. Who painted the 110-foot mural *The Age of Reptiles* displayed at Yale's Peabody Museum?

A. Rudolph F. Zallinger.

🌳

Q. In what year did Connecticut resident Frank McCourt win the Pulitzer Prize for biography?

A. 1997.

🌳

Q. What best-selling novelist is a 1982 graduate of Wesleyan University?

A. Peter Blauner.

Q. What Connecticut insurance company has a significant collection of American impressionist art?

A. Hartford Steam Boiler Inspection and Insurance Co.

Q. Who was the architect for the Old State House in Hartford?

A. Charles Bulfinch.

Q. What Connecticut museum has a collection of costumes from Diaghilev's Ballets Russes (Russian Ballet)?

A. Wadsworth Atheneum.

Q. Hartford's 1807 Center Church is modeled after what famous church in London?

A. St. Martin-in-the-Fields.

Q. What Connecticut structure is called the world's largest art deco design?

A. The Merritt Parkway.

Q. Hartford's Old State House houses a famous original portrait of George Washington by what artist?

A. Gilbert Stuart.

Q. What Connecticut county is noted for having created influential furniture styles in the eighteenth century?

A. New London County.

Q. How many libraries are there on the Yale University campus?

A. Twenty-one.

🌳

Q. Who was the director of the 1927 Wadsworth Atheneum, who encouraged experimentation in modern art, music, and dance?

A. A. Everett "Chick" Austin Jr.

🌳

Q. What Connecticut museum boasts sixty works by members of the Ash Can School?

A. New Britain Museum of American Art.

🌳

Q. How large are the audiences at the Sunken Garden Poetry Festival in Farmington?

A. Around three thousand.

🌳

Q. What Connecticut native was a convicted murderer and also a major contributor to the *Oxford English Dictionary*?

A. Dr. William Chester Minor.

🌳

Q. How many Connecticut theaters have won Tony Awards for their productions?

A. Six (the most of any state).

🌳

Q. What children's school magazine has long had its editorial offices in Connecticut?

A. *My Weekly Reader.*

Q. What city is host to the two-week International Festival of Arts & Ideas?

A. New Haven.

Q. Hartford's Wadsworth Atheneum has the largest collection of landscape paintings from what school of artists?

A. Hudson River School.

Q. Who was the Hartford-based literary scholar who was the first to propose that Shakespeare's works may not have been written by Shakespeare?

A. Delia Salter Bacon.

Q. What Connecticut museum combines a fine art gallery and a collection of carousel art?

A. Carousel Museum of New England, Bristol.

Q. How many copies of New Haven–born Dr. Benjamin Spock's *Baby and Child Care* have been printed?

A. Approximately fifty million.

Q. America's first degree-granting music school, Music Vale Seminary, was founded in 1835 in what town?

A. Salem.

Q. What Connecticut city hall features one of the largest collections of WPA murals from the 1930s and 1940s?

A. Norwalk.

Q. What is the name of the international storytelling event begun in 1988 by Connecticut Storytelling Center member J. G. Pinkerton?

A. Tellabration!

🌳

Q. What Connecticut city was the home of Harriet Beecher Stowe, author of *Uncle Tom's Cabin*?

A. Hartford.

🌳

Q. Hartford's performing arts center called the Bushnell was designed by the same architectural firm that designed what famous music hall?

A. Radio City Music Hall, New York City.

🌳

Q. What architect designed the colonial revival home, now known as Hill-Stead Museum, for her parents?

A. Theodate Pope.

🌳

Q. Who was the Hartford-born educational reformer who founded the *American Journal of Education*?

A. Dr. Henry Barnard.

🌳

Q. How many museums constitute Connecticut's Impressionist Art Trail?

A. Eleven.

🌳

Q. What architect, a Waterbury native, designed research centers for Bell Labs and IBM?

A. Ralph Thomas Walker.

Q. What are the three major professional theaters in New Haven?

A. Long Wharf, Shubert, and Yale Rep.

Q. In what town did Pulitzer Prize–winning poet and novelist James Merrill have a home?

A. Stonington.

Q. What is the name of the five-panel mural by Thomas Hart Benton on display at the New Britain Museum of American Art?

A. *The Arts of Life in America.*

Q. What is the name of the National Register Landmark that was the boyhood home of Eugene O'Neill?

A. Monte Cristo Cottage.

Q. What is the name of the world's tallest building, designed by New Haven architect Cesar Pelli?

A. Petronas Towers, in Kuala Lumpur, Malaysia.

Q. In what year did Connecticut-born Charles Ives win the Pulitzer Prize for his Third Symphony?

A. 1947.

Q. Laura Wheeler Waring of Hartford painted a portrait displayed in the National Gallery of Art of what famous fellow African-American?

A. W. E. B. DuBois.

Q. Lyman Beecher, father of author Harriet Beecher Stowe, was a Congregational minister in what town?

A. Litchfield.

Q. Marine and landscape painter Henry Pember Smith was born in 1854 in what town?

A. Waterford.

Q. In what year did Middletown host the annual traveling literary tournament called the National Poetry Slam?

A. 1997.

Q. What American portrait artist was a native of Guilford and lived for a time in the home of Samuel L. Clemens?

A. Mary Foote.

Q. Who was the landscape painter who depicted the Charter Oak some ten years before it was destroyed in a storm?

A. Frederic Edwin Church.

Q. What architect designed the Soldiers and Sailors Memorial Arch in Hartford's Bushnell Park?

A. George Keller.

Q. What award-winning African-American playwrights have a long association with the Yale Repertory Theatre?

A. Suzan Lori-Parks and August Wilson.

Q. In what year did the *Hartford Courant* begin publication?

A. 1764 (as the *Connecticut Courant*).

Q. Mark Van Doren, Pulitzer Prize–winning poet, novelist, critic, and teacher, had a farm in what Connecticut town?

A. Cornwall.

Q. Meryl Streep, Michael Douglas, and Al Pacino all studied at what Connecticut program?

A. The National Playwrights Conference, Waterford.

Q. What Connecticut town has trademarked the slogan "The Antiques Capital of Connecticut"?

A. Woodbury.

Q. The barn of what noted sculptor was the original gathering place for the "Knockers Club," later the Silvermine Guild of Artists?

A. Solon Borglum.

Q. What Connecticut-based author was the first to submit a typewritten manuscript to a publisher?

A. Mark Twain (the book was *The Adventures of Tom Sawyer*).

Q. Middletown composer Henry Clay Work wrote what popular song in 1876 that led to a new term in the language?

A. "Grandfather's Clock" (previously called a "tall case clock").

Q. New London was the birthplace of what noted American playwright?

A. Eugene O'Neill.

Q. In what year was Middletown's Wesleyan University founded?

A. 1831.

Q. What Connecticut woman was publisher of the *Connecticut Courant* (now the *Hartford Courant*) during the American Revolution?

A. Hannah Watson.

Q. In what year was the first public library in America established in New Haven?

A. 1656.

Q. Prize-winning playwright Arthur Miller has long been a resident of what Connecticut town?

A. Roxbury.

Q. The artistic school known as Cos Cob Impressionism was centered in what town?

A. Greenwich.

Q. The Connecticut Impressionist Art Trail was officially designated one of the fifty Millennium Legacy Trails by whom?

A. First Lady Hillary Rodham Clinton.

Q. What Hartford resident, widowed in 1862, was a noted patron of the arts in the late nineteenth and early twentieth century?

A. Elizabeth Colt (Samuel's wife).

Q. The Stamford Center for the Arts operates what two performance venues?

A. The Palace Theatre and the Rich Forum.

Q. The Stonington home of artist James McNeil Whistler was later the home of what American poet?

A. Stephen Vincent Benet.

Q. What internationally renowned theatrical director and teacher headed the Yale School of Drama and the Yale Repertory Theatre?

A. Lloyd Richards.

Q. What is the architectural style of the original 1844 building of the Wadsworth Atheneum?

A. Gothic revival.

Q. The Victorian garden at Hartford's Butler-McCook House was designed by what pioneering landscape architect?

A. Jacob Weidenmann.

Q. What Connecticut town is host to the annual National Puppetry Conference?

A. Waterford.

Q. What Connecticut town was the longtime home of artist and bird expert Roger Tory Peterson?

A. Old Lyme.

Q. The Wadsworth Atheneum displays an 1873 Renoir painting which depicts what other artist painting in his garden?

A. Claude Monet.

Q. The Wadsworth Atheneum displayed the country's first exhibit of surrealist art in what year?

A. 1931.

Q. Westbury is the home town of what noted American portrait photographer?

A. Annie Leibovitz.

Q. What 1810 Yale graduate was a painter of miniatures and an art teacher and helped found the National Academy of Design?

A. Samuel F. B. Morse (the inventor of the telegraph).

Q. What abstract expressionist made Greenwich his home in the latter years of his life?

A. Robert Motherwell.

Q. What Connecticut museum includes not only fine art but also a button museum?

A. Mattatuck Museum, Waterbury.

Q. What artist, a longtime resident of Connecticut, produced 210 covers for the *New Yorker* magazine?

A. Arthur Getz.

Q. First performing in 1895, what is the fourth-oldest symphony orchestra in the United States?

A. New Haven Symphony Orchestra.

Q. How many seventeenth-century tapestry panels of Psyche are on display at the Wadsworth Atheneum?

A. Five.

Q. What Hartford resident was the first African-American poet to be published, with "The Kind Master and the Dutiful Servant" in 1760?

A. Jupiter Hammon (or Hammond).

Q. What Hartford-based museum is the oldest public art museum in the country?

A. The Wadsworth Atheneum.

Q. Founded in 1903, what is the first museum in the country strictly devoted to American art?

A. New Britain Museum of American Art.

Q. How many venues for the performing arts are on the University of Connecticut campus at Storrs?

A. Four.

Q. How many works of art are in the permanent collection of the Wadsworth Atheneum?

A. Around fifty thousand.

Q. What Connecticut museum was once the center of a colony of American impressionist artists?

A. Florence Griswold Museum, Old Lyme.

Q. What Connecticut town has an annex of its public library at the town transfer station (the town dump) for recycling books?

A. Ashford.

Q. What Connecticut-born Yale graduate wrote the patriotic epic *The Columbiad*?

A. Joel Barlow.

Q. What early book is the prize holding of Yale's Beinecke Rare Book and Manuscript Library?

A. The Melk copy of the Gutenberg Bible.

Q. What eighteenth-century furniture maker is renowned for his vine tracery and large-scale base and scroll pediments?

A. Samuel Loomis of Colchester.

Q. Who hosts the annual National Playwrights Conference, held annually since 1965?

A. The Eugene O'Neill Memorial Theatre Center, Waterford.

Q. What Elizabeth Speare young-adult story is set in the Connecticut Colony of the late 1600s?

A. *The Witch of Blackbird Pond.*

Q. What famous American author wrote his most important works while living in Hartford?

A. Mark Twain (Samuel L. Clemens).

Q. What Hartford native and financial genius was the leading art collector of his day?

A. J. Pierpont Morgan.

Q. What Hartford native designed the grounds that surround the U.S. Capitol in Washington, D.C.?

A. Frederick Law Olmsted.

Q. In what Hartford neighborhood are the houses of authors Harriet Beecher Stowe and Mark Twain?

A. Nook Farm.

Q. What Hartford-born landscape artist is known for his paintings of the Andes and Niagara Falls?

A. Frederic Edwin Church.

Q. What historic house in Suffield has a rare display of eighteenth-century French wallpaper?

A. The Hatheway House.

Q. Who is quoted as saying, "Of all the beautiful towns it has been my fortune to see, [Hartford] is the chief"?

A. Mark Twain (after his first visit).

Q. What historic site was a boarding house for some two hundred artists during the period 1890–1920?

A. The Bush-Holley House, Greenwich.

Q. What institution sponsored choreographer George Balanchine's immigration to America in 1933?

A. The Wadsworth Atheneum.

Q. What internationally renowned playwright and author, a Yale graduate, had his home in Hamden?

A. Thornton Wilder.

Q. What is the architectural style of the state capitol in Hartford?

A. Victorian gothic.

Q. Who is the Connecticut-born and Yale-educated playwright, novelist, and noted AIDS activist?

A. Larry Kramer.

Q. What is the date of the oldest American work of art held by the Wadsworth Atheneum?

A. 1664.

Q. What is the date of the oldest work on display at the New Britain Museum of American Art?

A. 1740 (John Smibert's portrait of Benjamin Colman).

Q. What is the location of the Guilford Handcrafts Expo, the juried arts festival held annually in July?

A. The town green in Guilford.

Q. What is the museum on the campus of the University of Connecticut, Storrs, that serves as the Connecticut State Art Museum?

A. William Benton Museum of Art.

Q. What is the name of Foxwoods Casino's signature twelve-foot-tall sculpture of a Native American archer aiming into the sky?

A. *Rainmaker.*

Q. Who is the Hartford-born man who designed New York's Central Park?

A. Frederick Law Olmsted.

Q. What is the name of the thirty-thousand-volume fine arts library housed at the Wadsworth Atheneum?

A. Auerbach Art Library.

Q. What is the oldest university art gallery in North America, founded in 1832?

A. Yale University Art Gallery.

Q. What is the place of residence of noted columnist, novelist, and commentator William F. Buckley Jr.?

A. Stamford.

Q. What is the Pulitzer Prize–winning novel by William Styron, a longtime resident of Roxbury?

A. *The Confessions of Nat Turner.*

Q. What is the thickness of the translucent marble "panes" on the exterior of Yale's Beinecke Rare Book and Manuscript Library?

A. 1.25 inches.

Q. What Kent-based painter depicted twelve hundred species of birds in watercolors, now collected at the Connecticut State Museum of Natural History?

A. Rex Brasher.

Q. What late eighteenth-century literary group, known for its verse satires, were based in Connecticut?

A. The Hartford (or Connecticut) Wits.

Q. What later U.S. president taught history at Wesleyan University from 1888 to 1890?

A. Woodrow Wilson.

Q. Who has sponsored the acclaimed annual Art of the Northeast exhibition since 1948?

A. Silvermine Guild Arts Center, New Canaan.

Q. Who were the two noted journalists and brothers who were born in Avon, Connecticut?

A. Joseph and Stewart Alsop.

Q. Where is the home of the Connecticut Storytelling Festival, held annually in April?

A. Connecticut College, New London.

Q. Where is the largest collection of British art outside the United Kingdom?

A. Yale Center for British Art, New Haven.

Q. What Meriden-born operatic diva, discovered by Caruso, became a star at the Metropolitan Opera?

A. Rosa Ponselle.

Q. Where is the largest Waterford crystal chandelier in America on display?

A. Crystal Mall, Waterford.

Q. What Connecticut town is often referred to as "The Antique Capital of New England"?

A. Putnam.

Q. What minimalist artist was paid $87,000 in 1977 for Hartford's *Stone Field Sculpture,* an arrangement of thirty-six boulders?

A. Carl Andre.

Q. What museum features a permanent display of Coventry glass, a prized collectible that was made in Connecticut?

A. Strong-Porter House, Coventry.

Q. Where is the Nathaniel Jocelyn portrait of Cinque, the leader of the Amistad slave revolt?

A. New Haven Colony Historical Society.

Q. What museum is host to the renowned summertime series called the Sunken Garden Poetry Festival?

A. Hill-Stead Museum, Farmington.

Q. What music festival in Falls Village is the nation's oldest continuing summer chamber music event?

A. Music Mountain.

Q. Where is the National Critics Institute, a program for theater critics and arts writers, held annually in July?

A. The Eugene O'Neill Memorial Theatre Center, Waterford.

Q. Where is the only garden in America planned by famed English garden designer Gertrude Jekyll?

A. Glebe House Museum, Woodbury.

Q. Where was the first performance of what later came to be known as the New York City Ballet?

A. Hartford (sponsored by the Wadsworth Atheneum).

Q. What New Haven church was the first in the country designed in the gothic revival style?

A. Trinity Church.

Q. What New London museum is one stop on the Connecticut Impressionist Art Trail?

A. The Lyman Allyn Museum of Art.

Q. What Norwich museum sponsors an annual exhibition for Connecticut artists?

A. Slater Memorial Museum.

Q. What noted abstract expressionist taught at Yale University in 1962?

A. Helen Frankenthaler.

Q. What noted African-American contralto spent her retirement on a farm in Danbury?

A. Marian Anderson.

Q. What noted Danbury composer made his living selling insurance and wrote his music on weekends?

A. Charles Ives.

Q. Where can one find a recreation of Sherlock Holmes's sitting room at 221B Baker Street?

A. Gillette Castle, Hadlyme.

Q. Where can one see full-size plaster casts of famous classical and Renaissance sculptures?

A. Slater Memorial Museum, Norwich.

Q. What Old Lyme sculptor created the statue of Eugene O'Neill displayed at City Pier in New London?

A. Norman Legassie.

Q. Where can one view original works including Monet's *Haystacks* and Degas' *Dancers in Pink*?

A. Hill-Stead Museum, Farmington.

Q. Where did novelist Leo Tolstoy's son settle after leaving Russia following the 1917 revolution?

A. Southbury.

Q. Where did the New York Philharmonic perform their first outdoor concert in 1937?

A. The Silvermine Guild Arts Center, New Canaan.

Q. Where does author-illustrator Maurice Sendak have a home in the Connecticut woods?

A. Ridgefield.

Q. Where does New York's Whitney Museum have a Connecticut branch offering exhibits from its permanent collection?

A. Stamford.

Q. What one-time Waterbury resident painted *Harbor at Boulognes,* which is displayed at New York's Metropolitan Museum of Art?

A. Henry Golden Dearth.

🌳

Q. What Pulitzer Prize–winning American poet was also an insurance executive in Hartford?

A. Wallace Stevens.

🌳

Q. What Pulitzer Prize–winning author was a professor of English at Wesleyan University from 1959 to 1995?

A. Paul Horgan.

🌳

Q. What Redding resident (1908–1910) founded its public library?

A. Mark Twain.

🌳

Q. What renowned American photographer had a home in West Redding, Connecticut?

A. Edward Steichen.

🌳

Q. What Stamford establishment features acres of "recycled" architectural elements and antiques acquired from estates worldwide?

A. United House Wrecking Co.

🌳

Q. What style of architecture and design is featured at the Bushnell in Hartford?

A. Art deco.

Q. What town is home to the Yale Summer School of Music and Art, at the Stoeckel Estate?

A. Norfolk.

Q. What waggish phrase has been used to describe the state capitol in Hartford?

A. "The most beautiful ugly building in the world."

Q. What was the country's first mill to produce woolen cloth, in 1788?

A. Hartford Woolen Company.

Q. What was the name of Mark Twain's home in Redding, where he died in 1910?

A. Stormfield.

Q. What was the original name of Hartford's Trinity College?

A. Washington College.

Q. What Waterbury-born artist was a pioneer in the technique of color lithography?

A. Jacob Kainen.

Q. What Waterbury-born author proposed the emancipation of all slaves in 1776?

A. Samuel Hopkins.

Q. What Wilton country retreat was host to artists including Childe Hassam and John Singer Sargent?

A. Weir Farm.

🌳

Q. When did West Hartford's Noah Webster complete his first American dictionary?

A. 1806 (*A Compendious Dictionary of the English Language*).

🌳

Q. When Mark Twain first came to Hartford in 1868, whom did he come to visit?

A. Elisha Bliss of the American Publishing Co.

🌳

Q. When was the first children's library in the country established in Salisbury?

A. January 1803.

🌳

Q. Where can one enjoy summertime beachfront concerts of classical, pop, and jazz music?

A. Harkness Memorial State Park, Waterford.

🌳

Q. Where does noted fashion designer Diane von Furstenberg have a Connecticut home?

A. New Milford.

🌳

Q. Where is Whistler's father (George Washington Whistler), the father of artist James McNeil Whistler, buried?

A. Evergreen Cemetery, Stonington.

Q. Who created most of the hand-carved oak pews in Hartford's Trinity College Chapel, which required more than thirty years of work?

A. Gregory Wiggins.

Q. Who wrote the first American cookbook, published in Hartford in 1796?

A. Amelia Simmons.

Q. Whose collection of European decorative arts was acquired in 1917 by the Wadsworth Atheneum?

A. J. Pierpont Morgan.

Q. What Manchester company created museum-quality decorative textiles through its one hundred-plus-year history?

A. Cheney Brothers Mills.

Q. What Massachusetts college did Connecticut-born lexicographer Noah Webster found?

A. Amherst College.

Q. Whose gift of books in 1647 led to the founding of the New Haven Free Public Library?

A. Theophilus Eaton.

Q. Whose interior design firm decorated the first floor of the Mark Twain House in Hartford?

A. Lewis Comfort Tiffany's.

Q. What institution is the home for Connecticut's Center for Oral History?

A. Thomas J. Dodd Research Center at the University of Connecticut, Storrs.

Q. Who was the Hartford man who was the benefactor of the Wadsworth Atheneum?

A. Daniel Wadsworth.

Q. What was Connecticut's ranking in 2001 among all U.S. states for per capita spending on the arts?

A. First.

SPORTS & LEISURE

Q. Chris Smith, the University of Connecticut's (UConn) career scoring leader with 2,145 points, is a native of what city?

A. Bridgeport.

Q. Donyell Marshall, UConn's highest-ever pick in the NBA draft, was what selection in the 1994 draft?

A. Number four.

Q. Former UConn center Travis Knight won an NBA championship with what team?

A. Los Angeles Lakers (2000).

Q. Hartford-born Jim Murray, Pulitzer Prize–winning sports columnist for the *Los Angeles Times,* also received what other high honor?

A. He was inducted into the Baseball Hall of Fame.

Q. How many of Connecticut's state-maintained boat launching sites have saltwater access?

A. Twenty-five.

Q. What was the date of the last game for the Hartford Whalers NHL franchise?

A. April 13, 1997.

Q. Hiking trails in Connecticut state parks are marked by blazes of what color?

A. Blue.

Q. How many AA professional baseball teams are based in Connecticut?

A. Three.

Q. How many annual visitors are there on average at Hammonasset Beach State Park?

A. 1.5 million.

Q. How many Connecticut state forests have designated trails for snowmobiling?

A. Ten.

Q. How many fishing licenses are processed annually by the state of Connecticut?

A. Approximately 200,000.

Q. Aside from huge summer "cottages," what else is located in Connecticut's tiny borough of Fenwick?

A. A nine-hole golf course.

Q. How many overnight camp areas for canoeists are maintained by the state along the Connecticut River?

A. Three.

Q. How many polo clubs are based in Connecticut?

A. Seven.

Q. In Connecticut, what is a common term for what is generally called a submarine sandwich?

A. Grinder.

Q. In the long series of bulldog mascots at Yale, which one was the only female?

A. Handsome Dan XII (also called Bingo).

Q. How many public golf courses are there in Connecticut?

A. 102.

Q. In the New Haven area, what is the variant form of what is elsewhere called pizza?

A. Apizza.

Q. In what league did the New England Whalers (later the Hartford Whalers) first play?

A. World Hockey Association (WHA).

Q. In what month is the early duck hunting season in Connecticut?

A. October.

Q. How many state-maintained campsites are located in Connecticut?

A. Around fourteen hundred.

Q. In what year did the hockey franchise that became the Hartford Whalers begin operation?

A. 1972 (as the New England Whalers).

Q. In what year did the UConn women's field hockey team rank No. 1 in the country?

A. 1999.

Q. In what year did the Southern Connecticut State University Owls win their first of several men's NCAA Division II national soccer championships?

A. 1987.

Q. How many tennis coaches has Yale had in its 113-plus years of playing the sport at the varsity level?

A. Four.

Q. What is the only university to have both its men's and women's teams ranked No. 1 in the country at the same time?

A. The University of Connecticut (in basketball).

Q. In what year did the University of Connecticut women's basketball team win their first NCAA title?

A. 1995.

Q. How many trout hatcheries are run by the state of Connecticut?

A. Two.

Q. In what year did Yale start the first college boat club in America?

A. 1843.

Q. How many holes of golf are available at Middlefield's Lyman Orchards' courses?

A. Thirty-six.

Q. How many of Connecticut's state parks and forests have swimming facilities?

A. Twenty.

Q. In what years has the University of Connecticut men's soccer team won the NCAA Division I National Championship?

A. 1981 and 2000.

Q. The Hartford Wolf Pack are affiliated with what NHL hockey club?

A. New York Rangers.

Q. In what years has Yale won the Ivy League title in men's basketball?

A. 1957 and 1962.

🌳

Q. Mohawk Ski Area in Cornwall was the first in the country to make artificial snow during what dry winter season?

A. 1948–49.

🌳

Q. In what year did Yale students, playing on the New Haven Green, invent the toy later called the Frisbee?

A. 1920.

🌳

Q. Mrs. Frisbie's pies, whose pie plates led to the invention of the Frisbee, were made where?

A. Bridgeport.

🌳

Q. New York Yankee Cornelius "Neal" Ball, who completed the first unassisted triple play in baseball history on July 19, 1909, is buried where?

A. Mountain Grove Cemetery, Bridgeport.

🌳

Q. Old Saybrook is the home town of what NBA All Star?

A. Vin Baker.

🌳

Q. On September 16, 2000, the Yale football team became the first college team ever to achieve what?

A. Eight hundred victories.

Q. In what year did Yale win the first official Ivy League football championship?

A. 1956.

Q. On what day of the week is hunting not permitted by Connecticut state law?

A. Sunday.

Q. Salisbury boasts the second-oldest ski jump in the country, built in what year?

A. 1926.

Q. The Bridgeport Bluefish play baseball in what league?

A. Atlantic League.

Q. In what year did Yale's heavyweight varsity eight win the gold medal in rowing at the Olympics?

A. 1924.

Q. In what year was the first-ever collegiate mascot introduced at Yale ?

A. 1889.

Q. To whom did Babe Ruth present a copy of his autobiography at Yale Field in 1948?

A. Yale baseball captain (later U.S. president) George H. W. Bush.

Q. Trinity College of Hartford is the top sports program in the nation in what men's sport?

A. Squash.

Q. UConn star Corny Thompson of Middletown was selected by what NBA team in the 1982 draft?

A. Dallas Mavericks.

Q. What All-American player led University of Connecticut women's basketball to its first national title?

A. Rebecca Lobo.

Q. What annual Thanksgiving Day Connecticut road race attracts more than eleven thousand runners?

A. The Manchester Road Race.

Q. What baseball facility in Middletown has hosted several American Legion national tournaments?

A. William J. Pomfret Stadium at Palmer Field.

Q. What Bridgeport resident is considered the absolute authority on nineteenth-century baseball pitchers?

A. Frank Williams.

Q. What city hosted the Special Olympics World Games in 1995?

A. New Haven.

Q. What city is the birthplace of American League slugger Mo Vaughn?

A. Norwalk.

Q. What coach led the University of Connecticut men's basketball team to its first NCAA national title?

A. Jim Calhoun.

Q. What color are Connecticut hunters required to wear from September through February?

A. Fluorescent orange.

Q. What Connecticut cities had major-league baseball franchises in the 1870s?

A. Hartford, New Haven, and Middletown.

Q. What Connecticut city had an Eastern League minor-league baseball franchise from 1972 to 1982?

A. West Haven.

Q. What Danbury golf course has been rated among the top twenty-five public courses in the country?

A. Richter Park Golf Course.

Q. What direction should one look to get the best view of the "Sleeping Giant" in Hamden's Sleeping Giant State Park?

A. North.

Q. What event held annually in New London is the oldest inter-collegiate sports competition in America?

A. The Yale-Harvard Regatta, first held in 1852.

🌳

Q. What city is the birthplace of major-league pitcher Carl Pavano?

A. New Britain.

🌳

Q. What city is the hometown of professional and U.S.A. national team soccer star Carlos Parra?

A. West Haven.

🌳

Q. What former private summer residence is now a state forest set aside for public recreation?

A. Topsmead, in Litchfield.

🌳

Q. The New Britain Rock Cats are the AA minor league team affiliated with what major league baseball team?

A. The Minnesota Twins.

🌳

Q. What former UConn player has more than fifteen thousand career points in the NBA?

A. Cliff Robinson.

🌳

Q. What former Yale University president banned Pete Rose from baseball when he was commissioner?

A. A. Bartlett "Bart" Giamatti.

Q. What Hartford company manufactured the first American-made bicycles?

A. Weed Sewing Machine Co. (under contract to Albert A. Pope).

Q. What Hartford man was once president of Aetna Insurance and the first president of baseball's National League?

A. Morgan Bulkeley.

Q. What Connecticut city is the headquarters of sports network ESPN?

A. Bristol.

Q. The varsity sports teams at what Connecticut state university are nicknamed the Owls?

A. Southern Connecticut State University.

Q. What Connecticut city was the headquarters of the XFL professional football league?

A. Stamford.

Q. What high school did former New York Yankee outfielder Brian Dayett attend?

A. Valley Regional High School, Deep River.

Q. What is Connecticut's largest winter sports resort, with five chair lifts and twenty-three ski trails?

A. Mohawk Mountain, Cornwall.

Q. What is the common name in Connecticut for what is elsewhere called a garage sale or yard sale?

A. Tag sale.

Q. What is the full name of the basketball arena at the University of Connecticut, Storrs?

A. Harry A. Gampel Pavilion.

Q. What is the height of the aluminum dome that covers UConn's Gampel Pavilion?

A. 130 feet.

Q. What is the length of the greatest vertical drop at the Mohawk Mountain ski trails?

A. 640 feet.

Q. What Connecticut region is the saltwater fishing center of the state, with more than two dozen charter services available?

A. The New London area.

Q. What Connecticut resident won the Boston Marathon in 1957?

A. John J. Kelley.

Q. What is the length of the NASCAR-sanctioned race track at the Waterford Speedbowl?

A. One-third mile.

Q. What is the length of the oval track at Stafford Motor Speedway in Stafford Springs?

A. One-half mile.

Q. What is the longest golf hole in Connecticut?

A. The No. 18 at Yale Golf Course, a par 5 at 616 yards.

Q. What is the mascot for Connecticut College varsity sports teams?

A. The camel.

Q. What is the most popular species for sport fishing on the Thames River?

A. Striped bass.

Q. What is the name of the basketball court at UConn's Gampel Pavilion?

A. Alumni Court.

Q. What is the name of the greyhound track operating in Bridgeport?

A. Shoreline Star Greyhound Park.

Q. What Connecticut river is popular for whitewater kayaking?

A. The Housatonic River.

Q. The New Haven Ravens AA baseball franchise is affiliated with what major league team?

A. The St. Louis Cardinals.

Q. What Connecticut town boasts the most private golf courses, with seven?

A. Greenwich.

Q. What is the name of the indoor skating and hockey rink at Connecticut College in New London?

A. Dayton Arena.

Q. What is the name of the Lakeville race track that is regarded as the Road-racing Center of the Northeast?

A. Lime Rock Park.

Q. What is the name of the mascot of the Norwich Navigators baseball team?

A. Tater the Gator.

Q. The Norwich Navigators are the AA minor league team affiliated with what major league team?

A. New York Yankees.

Q. What Connecticut town is home to the state's only year-round greyhound track?

A. Plainfield.

Q. What Connecticut university won the NCAA Division III National Championship in baseball in 1998?

A. Eastern Connecticut State University.

Q. What is the name of the University of Connecticut mascot?

A. Jonathan.

Q. What is the nickname for the men's and women's varsity sports teams at Fairfield University?

A. The Stags.

Q. What is the oceanfront Donald Ross-designed public course, built in 1898?

A. Shennecossett Golf Course, Groton.

Q. What is the oldest international intercollegiate rivalry in the world, in which Harvard and New Haven's Yale compete against Oxford and Cambridge in tennis?

A. The Prentice Cup.

Q. What is the opening day of archery hunting season for wild turkey in Connecticut?

A. September 15.

Q. What is the opening day of muzzleloader hunting season for white-tailed deer in Connecticut?

A. December 5.

Q. What is the source of the steel in the metal wall in center field at Yale Field?

A. Old battleships.

Q. What Connecticut university, along with Amherst and Williams colleges, comprises the Little Three sports conference?

A. Wesleyan.

Q. What Connecticut-based company originally developed the design of K2 Skis?

A. Olin Corp.

Q. What lake in New Preston is the site of the Eastern Sprints rowing championship for women?

A. Lake Waramaug.

Q. What legendary New York Yankees broadcaster lived and is buried in Connecticut?

A. Mel Allen.

Q. What Middletown-based regatta is regarded as the largest single-day regatta in the Northeast?

A. The Head of the Connecticut Regatta.

Q. What New Haven resident is credited with writing the rules for American football?

A. Walter Camp.

Q. What New Haven–born golfer was dubbed the Female Bobby Jones?

A. Glenna Collett Vare.

Q. What New London park boasts an Olympic-size outdoor pool and a boardwalk along a saltwater beach?

A. Ocean Beach Park.

Q. What popular running event is held annually in Connecticut on the Fourth of July?

A. The Chester Road Race.

Q. What Shelton-based company is nationally known for its line of imported sporting knives?

A. Swiss Army Brands, Inc.

Q. What soccer star from Wilton had two goals and one assist for the 1999 World Cup champion U.S.A. team?

A. Kristine Lilly.

Q. What species of fish caught in the spring in the Connecticut River is considered a delicacy, despite its bony flesh?

A. American shad.

Q. What species of ocean fish cannot legally be fished in Connecticut waters?

A. Atlantic salmon.

Q. What stadium do baseball's Bridgeport Bluefish play in?

A. Harbor Yard.

Q. What Stamford brothers invented the first reciprocating model airplane engine in 1911?

A. The Echert brothers.

Q. What Stamford company was the country's leading maker of billiard tables in the 1870s?

A. H. W. Collender Co. (later merged into Brunswick).

Q. What star pitcher for the Cleveland Indians was born in Fairfield?

A. Charles Nagy.

Q. What state agency administers boating regulations and permits in Connecticut?

A. The Department of Environmental Protection.

Q. What Stratford man is said to have played every public golf course in the state?

A. Ed Crnic.

Q. What Stratford-based softball team won the women's national fast-pitch title six years in a row?

A. The Raybestos Brakettes.

Q. What three-sport star at UConn was American League Rookie of the Year with the Boston Red Sox in 1950?

A. Walt Dropo.

Q. What town bills itself as the hot-air ballooning capital of Connecticut?

A. Farmington.

Q. What town is Connecticut's most popular tourist destination?

A. Mystic.

Q. What town sponsors an annual Bluefish Festival, celebrating the locally popular saltwater game fish?

A. Clinton.

Q. What two Connecticut universities or colleges have varsity sports teams with Blue in their nicknames?

A. St. Joseph College (Blue Jays) and Central Connecticut State University (Blue Devils).

Q. What two Connecticut universities sponsor club teams in polo?

A. Yale and the University of Connecticut.

Q. What UConn All-American player was also a gold medalist for the U.S.A. basketball team in 2000?

A. Ray Allen.

Q. The New Haven Knights play in what minor hockey league?

A. United Hockey League.

Q. What UConn player was named the Most Outstanding Player of the 1999 NCAA Final Four basketball tournament?

A. Richard Hamilton.

Q. What USTA-sanctioned event is played annually in New Haven at the Connecticut Tennis Center?

A. The Pilot Pen Tournament.

Q. What was Killingworth resident Jeff Bagwell's batting average in his 1994 MVP season?

A. .367.

Q. What was the date of the first game ever played at the Yale Bowl?

A. November 21, 1914 (Harvard 36–Yale 0).

Q. What was the date of the first Yale–Princeton football game?

A. November 15, 1873.

Q. What was the final score when the Yale baseball team beat Wesleyan in 1865?

A. 39–13.

Q. What was the first season for UConn men's basketball coach Jim Calhoun?

A. 1986–87.

Q. What was the inaugural year for the women's crew team at Yale?

A. 1972.

Q. What was the length of Wyllys Terry's longest run from scrimmage for Yale in 1884?

A. 110 yards (the field was longer then).

Q. What was the name of the Bridgeport minor-league baseball franchise from 1902 to 1912?

A. Bridgeport Orators.

Q. What was the name of the Hartford major-league baseball team that played in the 1870s?

A. The Hartford Blues (or Dark Blues).

Q. What was the overall record of the University of Connecticut 1995 women's basketball team in their undefeated national championship season?

A. 35–0.

Q. What was the women's professional basketball team that starred UConn alumnae Jen Rizzotti and Kara Wolters?

A. The New England Blizzard.

Q. What was Wesleyan alumnus Bill Rodgers's best time in winning the Boston Marathon?

A. 2:09.27 (in 1979).

Q. What was Yale University's dual-meet record during the forty-year coaching career of legendary swimming coach Robert (Bob) Kiphuth?

A. 528–12.

Q. What Waterburian played on the first World Series championship team, the Boston Pilgrims in 1903?

A. George "Candy" LaChance.

Q. What Waterbury native and Baseball Hall of Famer was the Home Run King before Babe Ruth?

A. Roger Connor.

Q. What Waterbury YMCA official played on James Naismith's first organized basketball team in 1892?

A. William H. Davis.

Q. What were the years of existence of the Connecticut League in minor-league baseball?

A. 1902–12.

Q. What Wesleyan University alumnus won the Boston Marathon four times (1975; 1978–80)?

A. Bill Rodgers.

Q. Going to his classes the day after his victory, what Wesleyan University student won the Boston Marathon in 1968?

A. Amby Burfoot.

Q. What world-renowned bicycle company has its headquarters and design department in Bethel, Connecticut?

A. Cannondale.

Q. What Yale alumnus was a starting pitcher for the World Series–winning New York Mets in 1986?

A. Ron Darling.

Q. What Yale alumnus went on to become an NFL All-Pro and later coach of the Chicago Bears?

A. Dick Jauron.

Q. Who is the head coach of the two-time NCAA champion UConn women's basketball team?

A. Geno Auriemma.

Q. Who was the Russian-born All-American player for the UConn women's basketball team through the 2001 season?

A. Svetlana Abrasimova.

Q. What Yale grad and crew team member was quoted as saying, "Crew made me"?

A. Dr. Benjamin Spock.

Q. What Yale polevaulter was the first person ever to clear the heights of twelve, thirteen, and fourteen feet?

A. Arthur C. Gilbert.

Q. When did A. C. Gilbert invent the Erector Set, one of the most successful toys of the early twentieth century?

A. 1913.

Q. When was Connecticut's first blue-blazed hiking trail, the Quinnipiac Trail, opened?

A. 1929.

Q. Where are the Round Hill Highland Games held annually, with traditional Scottish competition?

A. Norwalk.

Q. Where did heavyweight boxer Gene Tunney, who defeated Jack Dempsey for the title, spend his retirement years?

A. Stamford.

Q. Where did major league pitcher Ricky Bottalico attend college?

A. Central Connecticut State University.

Q. Where did National League slugger Jeff Bagwell attend college?

A. The University of Hartford.

Q. Where do the AA Norwich Navigators play their home games?

A. Senator Thomas J. Dodd Memorial Stadium.

Q. Where has the Ox Ridge Charity Horse Show been held since 1914?

A. Ox Ridge Hunt Club, Darien.

Q. Where is the International Skating Center of Connecticut, a training facility for world-class figure skaters?

A. Simsbury.

Q. Where was baseball star and eccentric Jimmy Piersall, subject of the 1957 movie *Fear Strikes Out,* born?

A. Waterbury.

Q. Where was the first heavyweight title bout ever held in Connecticut?

A. Uncas Pavilion at Mohegan Sun.

Q. Which two species are hunted in Connecticut state forests as "big game"?

A. White-tailed deer and wild turkey.

Q. Who is the all-time leading scorer for UConn women's basketball?

A. Nykesha Sales.

Q. Who is the career leader in varsity starts for the UConn men's basketball team?

A. Jake Voskuhl, starting 135 games.

Q. Who is the leading ballcarrier in the history of UConn football, with 9,269 yards?

A. Matt DeGennaro.

Q. Who is the UConn women's soccer coach who was named National Coach of the Year in 1997?

A. Len Tsantiris.

Q. Who is the Yale alumnus who won the men's marathon at the 1972 Munich Olympics?

A. Frank Shorter.

Q. Who ranks as the all-time assist leader for the UConn men's basketball team?

A. Tate George.

Q. Who was the *Basketball News* National Defensive Player of the Year in the NCAA in 1998–99?

A. Ricky Moore.

Q. Who was the catcher for Hartford of the Eastern League in 1886?

A. Connie Mack.

Q. Who was the men's basketball coach who preceded Jim Calhoun at UConn?

A. Dom Perno.

Q. Who was the UConn player that led the nation in rebounds and rebound average in 1964–65?

A. Toby Kimball.

Q. Who was the UConn player who went on to win an NBA championship with the Chicago Bulls in 1998?

A. Scott Burrell.

Q. Who was the Waterbury native that served as Commissioner of Baseball from 1989 to 1992?

A. Francis T. "Fay" Vincent Jr.

Q. Who were the designers of the two golf courses at Middlefield's Lyman Orchards?

A. Robert Trent Jones and Gary Player.

Q. Woodstock resident Richard Johnson is a three-time Olympian (1992, 1996, 2000) in what sport?

A. Archery.

Q. Who was the coach for Southern Connecticut State University's NCAA Division II National men's soccer championship teams in 1998 and 1999?

A. Tom Lang.

Q. What Connecticut university holds the all-time record for most NCAA men's golf championships won?

A. Yale (twenty-one team titles).

Q. How many NCAA Division III national baseball championships have been won by Eastern Connecticut State University?

A. Three.

Q. What is the name of the golf course on which the Greater Hartford Open has been held in recent years?

A. River Highlands, in Cromwell.

Q. How many NCAA Division I national women's field hockey championships have been won by the University of Connecticut?

A. Two (1981 and 1985).

Q. How many visitors are there annually to the Mystic Seaport Museum in Mystic?

A. Nearly 400,000.

Q. What name is used for Moodus's Hale-Ray High School sports teams?

A. The Noises.

SCIENCE & NATURE

C H A P T E R   S I X

Q. What Connecticut native developed a revolutionary line of microcomputers?

A. Kenneth Olsen.

Q. Approximately how many trout are released annually by Connecticut's two trout hatcheries?

A. 800,000.

Q. Aside from dolphins, what other marine species performs at Mystic Marinelife Aquarium's Marine Theater?

A. Beluga whales.

Q. Aside from the Foxwoods Casino, what other major attraction is on the Mashantucket Pequot Reservation?

A. The Mashantucket Museum and Research Center.

Q. Capt. Nathaniel B. Palmer of Stonington is best known as the discoverer of what?

A. Antarctica.

Q. Connecticut leads the nation in the incidence of what infectious illness?

A. Lyme disease.

Q. Dr. Robert Ballard, discoverer of the wreck of the RMS *Titanic,* founded the Center for Undersea Exploration where?

A. Mystic Marinelife Aquarium.

Q. Edward Alexander Bouchet, the first African American to earn a doctorate, received his Ph.D. in physics from what university?

A. Yale University, in 1876.

Q. Famed photographer Edward Steichen developed a new hybrid of what flower at his Connecticut home?

A. Delphinium.

Q. What botanical oddity can one find at the Nut Museum in Old Lyme?

A. The world's largest nut, a thirty-five-pound coco-de-mer.

Q. What Bridgeport inventor developed the first (1878) American dirigible to carry a man in flight?

A. Charles F. Ritchel.

Q. What Bridgeport-born inventor developed the process of Polaroid instant photography?

A. Edwin H. Land.

Q. Hartford Electric Light Co. pioneered what industry electrical standard in the 1890s?

A. Sixty-cycle alternating current.

Q. Hartford native Horace Wells discovered what major advance in painless dentistry in 1844?

A. The anesthetic use of nitrous oxide (laughing gas).

Q. How many "field guides" were prepared by naturalist Roger Tory Peterson of Old Lyme during his lifetime?

A. Forty-five.

Q. In what year did the Great Hurricane devastate the Connecticut shoreline?

A. 1938.

Q. What Canterbury native introduced cataract removal surgery to the United States?

A. Mason Fitch Cogswell.

Q. When did Israel Putnam shoot the last timber wolf then remaining in the state of Connecticut?

A. 1742.

Q. When did Josiah Meiggs test an unmanned balloon, flying it across the New Haven Green?

A. 1785.

Q. What city was the birthplace of world-famous pediatrician Dr. Benjamin Spock?

A. New Haven.

Q. What graduate of Yale's Sheffield Scientific School patented the motorcycle in 1903?

A. George Selden.

Q. In what year did Yale alumnus Samuel F. B. Morse first demonstrate his invention, the telegraph?

A. 1844.

Q. How many different bird species have been recorded by Connecticut birdwatchers?

A. 399.

Q. How many different species of butterflies have been recorded in Connecticut's Butterfly Atlas?

A. 120.

Q. In what year did Yale University grant the first medical diploma in America?

A. 1729.

Q. What close friend of Simsbury native Gifford Pinchot helped him champion the cause of conservation at the turn of the century?

A. President Theodore Roosevelt.

Q. What former Hartford river was channeled into an underground conduit by the Army Corps of Engineers?

A. Park River.

Q. In what year was Catherine Beecher of the Hartford Female Seminary the first in the nation to teach domestic science and dietetics?

A. 1815.

Q. How many different species of ticks have been collected and identified in Connecticut?

A. Twenty-two.

Q. What company in Windsor Locks is the sole supplier of space suits to NASA?

A. Hamilton Sundstrand (formerly Hamilton Standard).

Q. What company was the first to make brass by direct fusion of copper and zinc, in 1802?

A. Abel Porter & Co., Waterbury.

Q. How many different varieties of roses are on display at Elizabeth Park in Hartford?

A. Nine hundred.

Q. In what year was Lyme disease first described in scientific literature in the United States?

A. 1977.

Q. How many natural history dioramas are on display at Yale's Peabody Museum?

A. Eleven.

Q. How many pounds of thrust are produced by the Connecticut-produced Pratt & Whitney PW 4098 jet engine, introduced in 1999 for the Boeing 777?

A. Ninety-eight thousand pounds.

Q. In what year was the first artificial heart pump, now in the Smithsonian, used at New Haven Hospital?

A. 1949.

Q. What is the total number of state forests in Connecticut?

A. Thirty.

Q. In what year was the first blast furnace in Connecticut opened in Lakeville?

A. 1762.

Q. How many rose bushes come to bloom in June at Hartford's Elizabeth Park?

A. Fourteen thousand.

Q. How many scientific specimens are in the collection of the Peabody Museum?

A. Around 11 million.

Q. In 1895 Connecticut inventor Curtis H. Veeder invented what device to measure distance traveled on a bicycle?

A. The cyclometer.

Q. In 1899 Hartford Electric Light Co. became the first in the world to use what in its transmission lines?

A. Aluminum wire.

Q. In what Connecticut city is the headquarters of aerospace company Pratt & Whitney?

A. East Hartford.

Q. What company, based in Groton, is the major submarine supplier to the U.S. Navy?

A. Electric Boat (division of General Dynamics).

Q. What Connecticut Aquarium features a 110,000-gallon shark aquarium?

A. The Maritime Aquarium at Norwalk.

Q. What Connecticut astronomer discovered a large asteroid orbiting the sun in October 2000?

A. Charles Baltay, Yale University.

Q. In what season are the largest number of bird species actually spotted at Hammonasset Beach State Park?

A. Fall.

Q. In what year did New Haven–born Charles Goodyear patent the vulcanization process for rubber?

A. 1844.

❦

Q. Mariangela Lisanti of Westport won a national competition for teens in 2000 by inventing what?

A. A device to measure conductance quantization in metallic nanowires.

❦

Q. New Haven–born Robert N. Hall invented a magnetron, the key operating component of what?

A. Microwave ovens.

❦

Q. New London's 1678 Joshua Hempsted House has insulation made of what natural material?

A. Seaweed.

❦

Q. What nonprofit organization coordinates public policy and education in the sciences in Connecticut?

A. The Connecticut Academy of Science and Engineering (CASE).

❦

Q. What noted American paleontologist established the huge fossil collection at Yale's Peabody Museum?

A. Othniel Charles Marsh.

❦

Q. What noted aviator was married in Noank in 1931?

A. Amelia Earhart.

Q. In what year was the state's first-in-the-nation Agricultural Experiment Station founded?

A. 1875.

Q. In what year was the world's first nuclear submarine, the USS *Nautilus,* launched at Groton?

A. 1954.

Q. On what downtown Hartford building do peregrine falcons have a nesting site?

A. Travelers Tower.

Q. Stamford resident Charles H. Phillips concocted and patented what product in 1873?

A. Milk of Magnesia.

Q. Stratford-born Kenneth Olsen invented what critical computer hardware component?

A. Magnetic core memory.

Q. What Connecticut city was the first in the nation to be fully lighted by electricity?

A. Hartford.

Q. What Connecticut company developed the computer-controlled equipment that can make eyeglass lenses in about an hour?

A. Gerber Scientific, Inc.

Q. What Connecticut inventor developed the world's first turbine-powered helicopter?

A. Charles H. Kaman.

Q. What did George C. Coy of New Haven build in 1878 out of bustle wires, teapot covers, and carriage bolts?

A. The world's first telephone switchboard.

Q. What East Hartford–built engine powered the Boeing B-50, the first airplane to fly nonstop around the world?

A. Pratt & Whitney's Wasp Major.

Q. What invertebrate is an endangered species in Connecticut?

A. Puritan tiger beetle.

Q. The Bowman Observatory is the home of the Astronomical Society of Greenwich and boasts a reflecting telescope of what diameter?

A. Twelve and one-half inches.

Q. The Connecticut Audubon Society sponsors nature programs at Trail Wood, the former home of what naturalist?

A. Edwin Way Teale.

Q. In what year was the world's first telephone exchange established in Bridgeport?

A. 1877.

Q. What is the name of the Connecticut state tree?

A. The white oak (Quercus alba).

Q. What Connecticut native built the *American Turtle,* the world's first submarine?

A. David Bushnell.

Q. What Connecticut science center features information on nuclear energy and medical uses of radiation?

A. Millstone Information and Science Center, Niantic.

Q. What Connecticut town is known for yielding valuable gemstones, such as the almandine garnet?

A. Roxbury.

Q. What Connecticut university appointed the first professor of paleontology in the United States?

A. Yale University.

Q. What Connecticut woolen merchant pioneered electric lighting in factories and the lead-acid battery as a backup for service outages?

A. Austin C. Dunham.

Q. What conservationist founded the Connecticut Audubon Society in 1898?

A. Mabel Osgood Wright.

Q. In what year was the worst-ever flood in Hartford, with the Connecticut River cresting at 37.5 feet?

A. 1936.

Q. The Connecticut River is an important spawning ground for what type of fish that includes shad and herring?

A. Anadromous fish (breed in freshwater but as adults live in saltwater).

Q. The first submarines manufactured in Groton (1924) were built for whom?

A. The Peruvian government.

Q. The GE scientist who invented Silly Putty in New Haven during World War II was trying to develop what?

A. Artificial rubber for tires.

Q. The state animal of Connecticut, Physeter catodon, is more commonly called what?

A. The sperm whale.

Q. What amateur naturalist founded the Connecticut Forestry Association in 1895?

A. Rev. Horace Winslow of Simsbury.

Q. What hospital pioneered the use of chemotherapy as a cancer treatment in 1942?

A. New Haven Hospital (now Yale-New Haven).

Q. What inventor and scientist, from his plant in Waterbury, pioneered cold strip mills for steel-making?

A. Tadeusz Sendzimir.

Q. What Essex man developed the formula for the world's most popular witch hazel, combining alcohol with the extract from the Hamamelis virginiana bush?

A. Rev. T. N. Dickinson.

Q. What is the best time to visit the Laurel Sanctuary in Union to see the state flower in bloom?

A. June and July.

Q. What is the diameter of the telescope at the Stamford Museum and Nature Center?

A. Twenty-two inches.

Q. What is the first and only air ambulance service operating in Connecticut?

A. Hartford Hospital's LIFE STAR helicopter.

Q. What Yale Medical School faculty member was one of the organizers of the American Medical Association in the 1840s?

A. Dr. Jonathan Knight.

Q. What Yale professor established the university as a major center of nineteenth-century scientific education?

A. Benjamin Silliman.

Q. What city is the site of a major research facility for Miles Laboratories, maker of Bayer Aspirin?

A. West Haven.

Q. The world-renowned Connecticut Forensic Science Laboratory is based in what city?

A. Meriden.

Q. The use of belting to transport steam power was invented by what Hartford man?

A. Pliney Jewell.

Q. What Yale Ph.D. and professor won the Nobel Prize for Chemistry in 1968?

A. Lars Onsager.

Q. Physiologist Roger Sperry, who won the Nobel Prize in 1981, attended what Connecticut high school?

A. William Hall High School, West Hartford.

Q. What is the oldest planetarium in Connecticut, built in 1954?

A. The University of Connecticut Planetarium, Storrs.

Q. What Yale-educated chemist studied the calorie content of food and developed the calorie tables still used today?

A. Wilbur Olin Atwater.

Q. When did Hartford Electric Light Co. demonstrate the world's first all-electric home?

A. 1908.

Q. When did naturalist Roger Tory Peterson, an Old Lyme resident, publish his first book, *A Field Guide to the Birds*?

A. 1934.

Q. When was Hartford's Institute of Living, one of the world's first behavioral health centers, established?

A. 1822.

Q. When was the first turbine-driven electrical generator in the country built, on Pearl Street in Hartford?

A. 1900.

Q. When was the Waldo Homestead black walnut tree, the largest in New England, planted, as recorded in the Waldo family bible?

A. 1797.

Q. Where can one board the *Sunbeam Express* for a whale-watching cruise off Long Island?

A. Waterford (at Capt. John's Dock).

Q. Where did David Bushnell test the *American Turtle,* the world's first submarine?

A. The Connecticut River.

Q. What is the name of Connecticut's only zoo, located in Bridgeport?

A. Beardsley Zoo.

Q. What Connecticut inventor is called the Father of Apparel Automation for producing the world's first fully automated cloth-cutting machine?

A. H. Joseph Gerber.

Q. Who was the first student at the country's first school for the deaf, established in Hartford in 1820?

A. Alice Cogswell.

Q. Yale-educated pharmacologist Alfred G. Gilman won the Nobel Prize in 1994 for his co-discovery of what?

A. G-proteins.

Q. Who won the 1989 Nobel Prize in Chemistry for his co-discovery of the catalytic properties of RNA?

A. Prof. Sidney Altman of Yale.

Q. What type of dolphins are featured in daily demonstrations at the Mystic Marinelife Aquarium?

A. Atlantic bottlenose dolphins.

Q. What type of organism causes the blight that has devastated Connecticut's chestnut trees?

A. A fungus.

Q. What university is the herbarium of record for the flora of southern New England?

A. University of Connecticut, Storrs.

Q. What University of Connecticut scientist was the first to clone cattle from cells grown in culture?

A. Dr. X. Jerry Yang.

Q. What was the increase in the number of national forests during the government service of Simsbury-born conservationist Gifford Pinchot?

A. From 32 to 149.

Q. Where was the world's first anaerobic sealant developed by Vernon and his son Robert Krieble, in 1953?

A. A basement laboratory at Trinity College, Hartford.

Q. The world's first fetal cardiovascular center was founded at Yale–New Haven Hospital in what year?

A. 1985.

Q. What was the name of the now-closed nuclear power plant at Haddam Neck?

A. Connecticut Yankee.

Q. What was the name of the U.S. Navy's first submarine, built in Connecticut in 1900?

A. *The Holland.*

Q. What Waterburian is one of the leading AIDS researchers in the world?

A. Dr. Robert Gallo.

Q. What West Hartford site features a full-size walk-in concrete model of a sperm whale?

A. The Science Center of Connecticut.

Q. What woodland species of canine began appearing in Connecticut for the first time in the 1950s?

A. The coyote.

Q. What Yale College rector constructed the first orrery (astronomical model) made in America?

A. Thomas Clap.

Q. What Yale graduates were the first Americans to see Halley's Comet in 1835, at the Yale Athenaeum Observatory?

A. Denison Olmsted and Elias Loomis.

Q. Where does the Nature Conservancy sponsor a bald eagle watch from December through March?

A. Shepaug Dam, Southbury.

Q. Where is Comstock, Ferre & Co., the oldest continuously operating seed company in the country?

A. Wethersfield.

Q. Where is Project Oceanology, whose "EnviroLab" research cruises teach oceanography, marine biology, and navigation?

A. University of Connecticut, Avery Point, Groton.

Q. Where is the oldest private songbird sanctuary in the United States?

A. Connecticut Audubon Birdcraft Museum, Fairfield.

Q. What is the name of the Wildlife Management Area (WMA) located in Burlington?

A. Sessions Woods.

Q. What Yale professor released the Environmental Sustainability Index in 2001, the most comprehensive study of the global environment?

A. Prof. Daniel C. Esty.

Q. Where is the Pinchot Sycamore, the largest and said to be the oldest tree in Connecticut?

A. Simsbury.

Q. Where was penicillin first used clinically in the United States, in 1942?

A. New Haven Hospital (now Yale-New Haven).

Q. Where was the first lobotomy in the country performed in 1939?

A. Hartford.

Q. What Lebanon-born physician is called the Father of Gastric Physiology for his studies of human digestion?

A. Dr. William Beaumont.

Q. What major pharmaceuticals company has its research laboratories based at a former submarine shipyard in Groton?

A. Pfizer, Inc.

Q. What Pratt & Whitney engine is the only one used to power all F-15 fighters?

A. The F-100.

Q. What research site is the largest physical possession of Yale University?

A. Yale-Myers Forest (7,800 acres).

Q. What Revolutionary War hero, born in Derby, introduced the Merino breed of sheep to Connecticut after serving as minister to Spain?

A. David Humphreys.

Q. Where were the first agricultural experimentation stations in the United States founded?

A. Wesleyan University (1875).

Q. Which Connecticut state forest included a rhododendron sanctuary for botanical study?

A. Pachaug, in Voluntown.

Q. John H. Van Vleck, a co-winner of the 1976 Nobel Prize in Physics, was born in what Connecticut city?

A. Middletown.

Q. Edward Kendall, 1950 winner of the Nobel Prize for his work on isolating hormones of the adrenal cortex, was born in what Connecticut town?

A. South Norwalk.

Q. Who invented the evaporation-condensation method for preserving milk?

A. Gail Borden of Torrington.

Q. Who is the Connecticut forensics expert who is regarded as the best in his field internationally?

A. Dr. Henry C. Lee.

Q. Who manufactured the first liquid-hydrogen engine to operate successfully in space?

A. East Hartford–based Pratt & Whitney.

Q. Who performed the first double-cross hybridization of corn, at the Connecticut Agricultural Experiment Station in New Haven?

A. Donald Jones.

Q. What Mansfield forest is a wildlife and wildflower sanctuary used as a University of Connecticut "classroom"?

A. Albert E. Moss Forest.

Q. What month on average is highest in precipitation in Connecticut?

A. March.

Q. What Mystic-based nature center includes a natural history museum, wildlife sanctuary, and educational summer camp?

A. Daniel Pequotsepos Nature Center.

Q. What name was given to the grouping of Yale science departments in 1861?

A. The Sheffield Scientific School.

Q. What New Haven man was the first person ever to set foot on Antarctica in 1822?

A. John Davis.

Q. What New Haven native invented the semiconductor injection laser, used in all CD players and laser printers?

A. Robert N. Hall.

Q. Who pioneered American research in probiotics, or the beneficial effect of certain bacteria for digestion and good health?

A. Yale's Dr. Leo Frederick Rettger.

Q. Who taught the first pediatric course in the nation at Yale Medical College in 1813?

A. Dr. Eli Ives.

Q. Who visited Hartford's Pope Manufacturing Co. several times in the 1890s to study their techniques of mass production?

A. Henry Ford.

Q. Who was the Bridgeport-born physicist who developed sheet polarizers, used in polarized lenses and LCD displays?

A. Edwin H. Land.

Q. What West Hartford native won the 1954 Nobel Prize for his pioneering discoveries about the virus that causes polio?

A. John Franklin Enders.

Q. What is the only amphibian that is an endangered species in Connecticut?

A. The Eastern spadefoot toad.

Q. What is the only mammal that is an endangered or threatened species in Connecticut?

A. The least shrew.

Q. What is the scientific name of the bacteria that cause Lyme disease?

A. Borrelia burgdorferi.

Q. Who was the bulldozer operator who uncovered 185-million-year-old dinosaur tracks in Rocky Hill in 1966?

A. Edward McCarthy.

Q. Who was the rival of Yale paleontologist O. C. Marsh during the "Fossil Feud" of the late nineteenth century?

A. Edward Drinker Cope.

Q. Who was the Suffield-born health-food advocate who promoted vegetarianism and the use of coarse whole-wheat flour in the mid-1800s?

A. Sylvester Graham (hence, graham crackers).

Q. What is the size of the Connecticut College Arboretum in New London?

A. Seven hundred acres.

Q. What two Connecticut educational institutions did Dickinson W. Richards, winner of the 1956 Nobel Prize for his work on heart disease, graduate from?

A. Hotchkiss School and Yale University.

Q. What Hartford-born scientist was awarded the Nobel Prize in 1983 for her discovery of mobile genetic elements?

A. Barbara McClintock.

Q. What Killingly native was the first woman to be granted a U.S. patent, in 1809?

A. Mary Kies.

Q. What school founded in West Cornwall in 1845 was the first agricultural school in the nation?

A. Cream Hill School.

Q. What species of bear is becoming more widespread in Connecticut?

A. Black bear.

Q. What species of bird is listed as of "special concern" in Connecticut because of a serious population decline?

A. The willet.

Q. What species of fish is an endangered species in Connecticut?

A. The shortnose sturgeon.

Q. What state park features dinosaur tracks that were fossilized in sedimentary rock?

A. Dinosaur State Park.

Q. What Stratford-based inventor developed the first successful helicopter in the United States?

A. Igor Sikorsky.

Q. What type of bridge is used to carry the Amtrak railroad tracks over the Connecticut River?

A. A bascule bridge.

Q. Who was the Woodstock-born author of the 1789 work *The American Geography*, regarded as the Father of American Geography?

A. Jedidiah Morse.

Q. Who was the Yale professor of forestry and pioneering environmentalist who coined the phrase "conservation of natural resources"?

A. Gifford Pinchot.

Q. Yale expeditions lead by Othniel Charles Marsh discovered and named what two dinosaur species?

A. Triceratops and Stegosaurus.

Q. Yale researchers Gifford Pinchot and Henry S. Graves were the first in America to demonstrate what conservation activity?

A. Forest management.